COMPANION INTO BUCKINGHAMSHIRE

Dorney Court : Dining Hall

COMPANION INTO
BUCKINGHAMSHIRE

By MAXWELL FRASER

*WITH FIFTEEN PLATES
AND ENDPAPER MAP*

SPURBOOKS LIMITED

First published by Methuen & Co. Ltd. in 1950

This edition, with a new endpaper map, by
Spurbooks Limited, 88 Blind Lane,
Bourne End, Bucks., 1972

Reprinted offset litho by Biddles Ltd., Guildford, Surrey.

SBN 0 902875 13 2

To

MR. ROBERT TAYLOR

Alderman of the county of Bucks
and of the Borough of Slough,
who shares my interest in the
county in which we live

AUTHOR'S NOTE

I HAVE to acknowledge with gratitude the help of clergy, local councils, pressmen and many others, among whom I owe special thanks to Mr. Robert Taylor for his kindness in reading through the proofs; Miss Margaret Beattie, County Librarian, Aylesbury, and Miss G. P. P. Knowles and staff of the Slough Public Library, who have been so sympathetic and unwearying in searching for specialized information. Col. Guy Crouch, the Clerk, and other officers of the County Council; Miss Cecily Baker, Archivist and Librarian of the Bucks Archæological Society, Mr. R. C. Sansome, Curator of the County Museum, and Mr. Nigel Viney, all of Aylesbury, have also been most helpful.

Special mention must be made of Miss Myra Hardcastle, of Observatory House, Slough, for information in regard to the Herschel family; the Rev. W. F. Palmer, of Langley Marish, the Rev. D. J. Jones, Hedgerley, the Rev. T. H. South, Amersham, and the Rev. A. J. Toomey, Clifton Reynes; Professor and Mrs. Grey Turner, Huntercombe Manor; Mr. S. W. Lord, Mrs. S. G. Soul, and Mr. T. R. Maynard, Olney; Mr. Alfred Duffield, Fenny Stratford, Mr. N. M. Fowler, Deputy Clerk to the Council, High Wycombe, and Mr. H. Berry, of Messrs. Harrison's Stamp Factory, High Wycombe. Mr. Edgar Phillips (Trefin of the Welsh Gorsedd) has kindly furnished information in regard to Celtic place-names.

Although there has been a great influx of people into the county since the first world war, particularly in the southeast, few of these newcomers have any knowledge of their adopted county, but in driving, bicycling, or walking over Buckinghamshire since my earliest days, I have found the older people interested in their county, and proud of its associations, and to these I give my thanks for much that cannot be found in books.

MAXWELL FRASER

CONTENTS

ILLUSTRATIONS

LONG before the coming of the Romans, men made their way up the Thames to settle on the fertile lands which lie between the river-bank and the Chiltern Hills, and to-day there is no more delightful introduction to south Buckinghamshire than its Thames-side towns and villages.

The river marks the southern boundary of Buckinghamshire, from the London Stone on the Middlesex border, to the Oxfordshire boundary, and in this thirty miles is crammed an epitome of the story of Britain. Buckinghamshire is reached a little over four hundred yards from the London Stone, which was set up at Staines in 1285, and marks the upper limit of the Lower Navigation, and the former limit of jurisdiction of the City of London. It is here the true Thames Valley can be said to commence, with the River Colne reaching the Thames near Bell Weir Lock, a favourite haunt of fishermen.

On the Surrey bank are the level fields of Runnymede, now in the care of the National Trust, to commemorate that momentous day when the Barons finally succeeded in bringing King John to book, and forced him to make his mark on the Magna Charta.

There is no record of the exact spot where the signing took place, but the generally accepted version is that the Barons and their great forces occupied the fields of Runnymede, whilst the King with his followers encamped on the Buckinghamshire shore, and that they met on the island between. A stone framed in oak, claimed to be that on which King John rested the parchment when he affixed his seal to Magna Charta, is preserved on Magna Charta Island.

The Ankerwyke estate, to which Magna Charta Island

belongs, is magnificently wooded, with splendid chestnut trees overhanging the river. A yew tree there is said to date from the time of King John, and to have been a trysting place of Henry VIII and Anne Boleyn. There are the remains of a Benedictine nunnery founded in the reign of Henry II, now very fragmentary. The Priory was valued at £132 0s. 2d. at the Dissolution, and was granted to Lord Windsor. Ankerwyke House was built in the early nineteenth century on the site of the residence of Sir Thomas Smith, a statesman and scholar whose father claimed descent from an illegitimate son of the Black Prince. He was appointed Provost of Eton in 1547, and was the author of many important works, his *De Republica Anglorum; the Maner of Government or Policie of the Realm of England* being the most important description of the constitution and government of England written in the Tudor period.

Wraysbury, or Wyrardisbury, became a royal manor early in the fourteenth century. The older part of the village is a pleasant enough little place, with some much-altered seventeenth-century buildings. The thirteenth-century church was practically rebuilt in 1862, by Raphael Brandon, who also rebuilt the church at the neighbouring village of Datchet, and gave each a stone spire. The plain whitewashed interior has a brass of John Stonor by the chancel steps, generally said to be clad as an Eton scholar, but now pronounced to be in the robes of a sixteenth-century doctor of laws. There is also a brass of a knight in Tudor armour, and a stone to Edward Gould, who was a servant of Charles II. There are also several interesting eighteenth-century monuments—interesting not so much for those they commemorate, as for their workmanship, which is so typical of the period.

North of the church is the seventeenth-century George Inn, where the Vestry once held its meetings. Wyrardisbury House was formerly the rectory, and Bowry Farm derives its name from a yeoman family who lived there in the seventeenth and eighteenth centuries. Close to the riverside are the Old Ferry House and Place Farm, the latter popularly known as King John's Hunting Lodge, but probably an early sixteenth-century house of timber framing, refaced at a later date. Wraysbury once had a wharf on the river bank where copper ore was landed, to be minted at the mill in Copper-mill Road, and then taken to London.

The newer part of Wraysbury chiefly consists of bunga-lows and caravans crowding as close to the river as possible.

Beyond Wraysbury the river winds with its willow-bordered banks to Datchet, where, although history may tell us of the many variations in the spelling of the village name from the tenth century onwards, it appears at first sight purely modern to the view. It is so delightfully grouped round its wide, smooth-lawned green that it is one of the most captivating of riverside resorts.

All but the chancel of the church was also rebuilt in the mid-nineteenth century, and the chancel itself was much altered. Some interesting old monuments remain, including a brass with an inscription and shield of arms to Katherine, wife of Sir Mores Berkeley, who died in 1559; and a rectangular brass plate, with the kneeling figures of Richard Hanbury, citizen and goldsmith of London, the date of whose death is not filled in, Alice his wife, who died in 1593, and two daughters. There are also several seven-teenth-century mural tablets and floor slabs. Three of the rich purple and red Victorian stained-glass windows are memorials to the Prince Consort.

Boating and angling are still the chief attractions of Datchet, as befits a place where those devoted fishermen, Sir Henry Wotton, Provost of Eton, and his friend Izaak Walton, once plied their rods. Sir Henry, described by Walton as 'a most dear lover and frequent practiser of the art of angling', built a fishing-house at Black Potts, where he was visited yearly by Walton, to whom he wrote in April 1639, the last year of his life, in anticipation of Walton's 'ever-welcome company in this approaching time of the fly and the cork'. Later, the painter Verrio built a summer-house on the site, where Charles II also fished, and Pope wrote:

> 'Methinks I see our mighty monarch stand
> The pliant rod now trembling in his hand;
>
> .   .   .   .
>
> And see he now doth up from Datchet come,
> Laden, with spoils of slaughter'd gudgeons, home.'

The summer-house, like Walton's fishing-house, has long vanished, but Black Potts is still a favourite haunt of anglers.

Isaac Penington, the Puritan and religious writer, lived at Datchet for a while before settling at Chalfont St. Peter in 1658, and William and Caroline Herschel in 1782, before they settled at Slough.

Christopher Barker, born at Datchet in 1529, was Queen's Printer to Elizabeth. A tablet in Datchet church records that he printed the Authorised Version of the Bible at his own expense. Another native of Datchet was Richard Clark, the musician, who was born there in 1780, of a musical family. His mother was the daughter of John Sale, the elder, a lay clerk of St. George's Chapel, Windsor, to which Clark was admitted at an early age as a chorister. He did excellent work in his endeavours to obtain for singing men and choristers of cathedrals the ancient privileges of which they had been deprived in the course of time.

There has been a ferry from Datchet to Datchet Mead, on the opposite side of the river, from 'time immemorial'. There are many references in the privy purse expenses to payment of ferrymen at Datchet, but when a public bridge, free of toll, was built in 1706, the ferry was discontinued. Datchet Mead is, of course, associated with a misadventure of

Falstaff in *The Merry Wives of Windsor*, and with the horse-races, founded by Charles II, which were the forerunner of Ascot.

The approach to Eton along the river is heralded by a glimpse of the south front of Eton College, framed in giant trees, and with greensward lapped by the quietly-flowing backwater, which has inspired many a painter with its peaceful beauty.

Eton's history is so bound up with that of the College that there is a tendency to forget it is far older. Eton was in existence before the Conquest, and is known to have attained its present limits by the thirteenth century, for the Hundred Rolls of 1275–6 refer to the *villata* of Eton from Baldewin Bridge to Windsor Bridge—and these bridges are still landmarks. The meadow beside the river, known as the Brocas, gained its name in the fourteenth century, when it was owned by John Brocas, surveyor of works in Windsor Castle.

Linked to the Royal Borough of Windsor by a bridge over the Thames, Eton seems redolent of the past—perhaps because its narrow High Street, the bane of the motorist, and the joy of the pedestrian, is in such complete contrast to the modern type of highway. Few main streets have a more fascinating situation than Eton's High Street, with the massive thirteenth-century Curfew Tower blocking the southern skyline, and the mellow beauty of Eton College to the north. There are houses of graceful late Georgian or early nineteenth-century architecture, and a few still older buildings, although only the Cockpit remains unaltered on the exterior. The Crown and Cushion and the Turk's Head are both of seventeenth-century work. The Cockpit, built before 1420, has the remains of an old cockpit, including the knucklebone floor, where tradition tells that Charles II was often a spectator.

Beyond the bridge over Barnes Pool, which marks the end

of High Street and the commencement of the College buildings, is an archway with plaster casts on the walls, opening
into the courtyard of Jourdelay's, which resembles an old
Dutch picture. The name of Jourdelay's commemorates the
name of the original owner of the site, which was purchased
by Henry VI from Thomas Jourdelay in 1441. The house
was a refuge for the 'ever-memorable' John Hales, when he
was ejected from his Eton Fellowship for his Royalist
sympathies, and he died there in 1656.

No school is more enchantingly situated than Eton, in its
spacious green playing-fields shaded by immemorial elms,
and there is an extraordinarily happy mingling of styles and
architectural design in the College buildings.

Henry VI was only eighteen years of age when he first
began to plan the College, and only twenty when he laid the
foundation stone of the Chapel on Passion Sunday, 1441.
Dr. Thomas Beckington, Archdeacon of Buckinghamshire,
was the prime mover in the tedious negotiations with the
Pope which resulted in the Bull authorising the Collegiate
Church. When he was rewarded with the Bishopric of Bath
and Wells, he was consecrated in the old Collegiate Church,
and gave a banquet in one of the new buildings of the
uncompleted college.

The letters patent of the founder provided for a provost,
ten priests (the Fellows), four clerks, six choristers, 'twenty-
five poor and needy scholars to learn grammer there', and
twenty-five poor and disabled men to pray for the souls of
his father and mother and all his forefathers, also a master or
informator in grammar. New statutes in 1443 established a
close relationship between Eton and King's College, Cambridge, which the king had founded two years previously.
The king wrote in a warrant on 3 June, 1446 'that the same
school as it surpasses all other such grammar schools what-
soever of our kingdom in the affluence of its endowment and
the pre-excellence of its foundation, so may it excel all other

grammar schools, as it ought, in the prerogative of its name, and be named therefore the King's General School, and be called the lady, mother, and mistress of all other grammar schools'.

Henry personally laid down instructions for the style and material of the buildings: 'Laying aparte superfluity of too curious works of entayle and busie mouldings, I will that both my sayd colleges be edified of the most substantial and best abyding stuffe', but most of his plans were modified or completely altered after his death. His plan to have a nave of 168 feet to the chapel was curtailed to the present building. The Lower School, which faces it across School Yard, is the original Eton schoolroom, and is probably the oldest school-room in continuous use in England, having been built not later than 1500. The Upper School, on the west side of School Yard, was completed in 1694, and Lupton's Tower, on the east, was built at the beginning of the sixteenth century. The Founder's Statue, in the centre of School Yard, was erected in 1719, and a tradition has arisen that it must always be kept on the left in passing. The bombing in 1940 fortunately damaged only the west front of School Yard, which has been skilfully restored.

The Hall, reached by a flight of steps on the south side of the cloisters, was one of the first portions of the founder's plan to be completed, and was probably in use by about 1450. Together with the Pantry and Kitchen, it was the only portion of the College which occupied the position laid down by Henry VI. Among many interesting particulars of the building furnished by the account books preserved at Eton, is proof that labour troubles were not confined to our own day, for more than once men got into trouble 'for late cuming', particularly after the mid-day meal. Many fines are recorded which throw a vivid light on the trials of the overseers—twenty-one men, due to return to work at one o'clock, forfeited a whole day's wages when 'they wolde not go to their work til twoo of clocke', and other fines were imposed for 'fyting' and for men who 'wrostled and playde and ron about', or 'wol not do nor labor but as he list hymselfe'.

There is a detailed guide to the college, by the Rev. R. A. Austen-Leigh, which does full justice to the many treasures of Eton, including the brasses, monuments, and unrivalled fifteenth-century wall paintings of the Chapel, and the splendid collection of illuminated MSS. and books in the library. There are many rare early English plays, valuable Shakespeareana, books and broadsides printed by early Master Printers, the first editions of *Paradise Lost*, Herrick's *Hesperides* and other notable books; one of the only three known copies of Kyd's *Spanish Tragedie*, dated 1602; the first edition of Dr. Johnson's *Dictionary*, lying on the Doctor's own desk; the Mazarin Bible, printed and illuminated in Germany about 1445, which was the first book printed from movable metal types and is one of the six existing copies in the original binding; a manuscript copy of the first English comedy, *Ralph Roister Doister*, written by Nicholas Udall, who was headmaster of Eton in the sixteenth century; a deed with the autograph of William Rufus, another with the earliest known picture of Windsor Castle, and many other rare treasures. A case 18 inches square contains no fewer than four hundred volumes of Japanese verse presented by the Emperor of Japan, and there are numerous autograph letters of Etonians of all periods.

The gentle, scholarly Founder loved to talk to the Eton boys, and always bestowed on them small—but doubtless very welcome—presents of money, saying, 'Be good boys, meek and docile, servants of the Lord'.

Many of the later Kings of England have taken a personal interest in the school, especially George III, who in his kindly way also chatted freely to the boys. He is affectionately remembered to this day by the celebrated Fourth of

June celebrations, which commemorate his birthday, and in the top hats and tail coats which were first worn as mourning at his death, in place of the eighteenth-century uniform of blue coat, knee-breeches, and white waistcoat.

The Wars of the Roses, not unnaturally, had an adverse effect on Eton. Although a document promising protection was obtained in 1461 from the victorious Edward, Duke of York, afterwards Edward IV, within a year he had not only taken away a large part of the endowment, but actually obtained a Bull from the Pope to dissolve the College founded by his rival. Fortunately, the Provost, William Westbury, persuaded the King to have the Bull dissolved. Earl Rivers, the King's brother, who was a great patron of learning, exerted himself on behalf of the College, and there is a tradition that Jane Shore also interceded on its behalf.

The setback, which might have been fatal, proved the highroad to success, for the Provost and Headmaster had to supplement their diminished salaries by admitting rich pupils, who paid fees and boarded with Fellows, or in the town of Eton, and were known as Oppidans, in contrast with the Collegers, or 'tugs', provided for by the Founder.

The Reformation was accepted without a dissentient voice, but once again the suppression of Eton was contemplated, and the College was only saved by the death of Henry VIII.

Henry, in his usual masterful way, compelled the College to take property in Kent and elsewhere, in exchange for a splendid site north and south of Piccadilly, which gave rise to the rhyming hexameter:

'Henricus Octavus took away from us more than he gave us'.

Most of the earlier Headmasters maintained discipline by flogging, but Nicholas Udall, William Malim and Dr. Keate appear to have achieved especial fame for their severity.

An account of the curriculum in the sixteenth century, left by William Malim, shows that the boys had a sufficiently hard life without these unmerciful beatings. They had to work ten hours a day, starting at six in the morning. There was an elaborate system of monitors or prepositores, among others 'Prepositores for yll kept hedys, unwasshid facys, fowle clothes, and sich other. Yffe there be iv. or v. in a howse, monytores for chydyng and for Laten spekyng'. Friday was a fast day, and all offences of the past week were enumerated and punished on this day. The only amelioration of their lot appears to have been the occurrence of feast days and the annual celebration of the Montem. There were also short holidays, but the boys were not allowed to go home.

A serious threat to the everyday life of the scholars grew up through a new practice of dividing the annual surplus of revenue among the Fellows and Provost, which appears to have provided an irresistible temptation to skimp in the seventeenth century, for Sir H. Maxwell-Lyte records in his *History of Eton College* 'in 1635 the scholars complain that they are robbed of breakfast, clothing, bedding, and the commonest necessities of life, while the college income is divided among the few'.

It was said in 1834 'the inmates of a workhouse or a gaol are better fed and lodged than the scholars of Eton'. There were not enough bedsteads in the notorious Long Chamber, so that some of the boys had to sleep on the floor between the beds. Most of the glass in the windows was broken, and there were no washbasins. The only provision for washing was the old pump in the cloister, and the dirt can be better imagined than described when it is realized that the only attempt at cleaning was made once a year, just before Election time—when alone visitors were allowed in the room. The cleaning took the form of 'rug-riding', when Lower boys were tied up in big rugs off the beds, and dragged up and down the floor by the older boys to polish it!

There was no supervision at all in Long Chamber, where seventy boys were locked in from 6.30 p.m. until the following morning. The amount of bullying depended solely upon the disposition of the Upper boys, and frequently went to appalling lengths. There were rat hunts, feasts of smuggled food, gambling and every amusement the fertile minds of the boys could devise.

Those who complain of overcrowding in modern schools would be astounded at the conditions prevailing for centuries at Eton. One schoolroom, known as the 'Cockloft', was 'a narrow loft with about a dozen tiers of seats, the uppermost so high that the boys seated on it could touch the ceiling. The forms were so low and so close to each other, that the boys sat with their knees higher than their waists; and the boys of each row rested their backs against the knees of those in the row behind. If a fellow came in late, he disturbed the whole form in climbing to his place, and if one on the upper tiers got a shove in the scrimmage that occurred when schooltime was over, he ran risk of a nasty fall.'

Another, called the 'Black Hole', was a little narrow room which was called upon to accommodate a hundred and fourteen boys. It 'could not, by any arrangement of seats—which were very small and fixed in slanting and sloping steps nearly up to the ceiling—nor by any thick packing, which was always a source of squabbling and contest among the boys, be made to hold more than about eighty, so that there were always about thirty in the doorway and sitting on the stairs, many of them out of sight, and, of course, out of command'.

The food, too, was bad. No breakfast was provided, and only mutton and mashed potatoes, in insufficient quantities, at dinner all the year round, with half a chicken and some greens to each boy on Founder's Day and Election Day as the only variation. In summer, when the hours of work were relaxed, the boys were allowed a siesta in the schoolroom after dinner, and wakened in time for a 'bever' of bread and beer, served at 3 p.m.

An account of the system of education pursued at Eton in the early part of the reign of George III was drawn up between 1768 and 1775 by Thomas James. It reveals a milder form of discipline than that under Malim, and some relaxation of the working hours, but conditions were still extremely bad until the reforms initiated in June, 1844, when additional sleeping accommodation was provided, and the Long Chamber divided into separate cubicles, and other sorely needed improvements made.

The extreme turbulence of the boys under such conditions makes the severity of the 'flogging Heads' more understandable. It is recorded that on more than one occasion the Headmaster was pelted with rotten eggs and subjected to other indignities which he was almost powerless to avert, owing to the impossibility of enforcing discipline on four or five hundred boys with only about half-a-dozen masters to assist him. Dr. Keate's prodigious floggings would seem to have justified themselves, for he succeeded in exacting order and obedience, and won the affection of the boys for the real kindness of heart and the dauntless courage which lay behind his gruff ways. On the celebrated occasion when he flogged over eighty boys in the same day, he was cheered—chiefly in admiration for such a feat; and when he retired in 1834 a large sum of money was subscribed to present him with a testimonial.

Eton has, of course, had many celebrated headmasters and provosts. Perhaps one of the most lovable of the latter was Sir Henry Wotton, who was, Izaak Walton tells us, 'a cherisher of all those youths in that School, in which he found either a constant diligence or a genius that prompted them to learning. . . .' The most original of the appointments was that of Richard Allestree, who had fought as a royalist soldier at the battle of Edgehill. It is said Charles II challenged one of his courtiers to show him an uglier man than himself, and when Allestree was produced, the King conferred upon him the vacant office. Allestree proved worthy of his new appointment, and built the Upper School at his own expense.

In spite of the appalling conditions under which the scholars lived—or possibly because of them—the College has contributed a larger proportion of the rulers of England than any other school. The Duke of Wellington, Pitt, Charles James Fox, Canning, Sir Robert Walpole, and Gladstone, are only a few of the great statesmen educated at Eton, and its record of scholars and men of letters, ambassadors, ecclesiastical dignatories, cabinet ministers and peers, is no less distinguished, whilst it furnished the country with great military leaders long before the days when 'the battle of Waterloo was won on the Playing Fields of Eton'.

The Eton Montem, which took place at Salt Hill, beside the Bath Road, was abolished after the opening of the railway, which brought crowds of rowdy and undesirable spectators.

The most important of the surviving customs is, of course, the Fourth of June, when the procession of boats takes precedence over all other festivities. Eton is a great centre for rowing, and the Captain of the Boats is considered of more importance than the Head of the School. Eton Fives is now played by other schools also, but the special form of football known as the Field Game, and the famous Wall Game, are peculiar to the College.

The origin of the Wall Game is not known with certainty, as there are few records of it before the nineteenth century. It is played on St. Andrew's Day, along a strip of ground bordered by a wall built in 1717, with a tree at one end, and the door of Weston's Yard at the other for goals. It is extremely difficult for an onlooker to follow the game, with its complicated rules. The score is said to average about three goals in a hundred years!

The Eton Society, or Pop, which now maintains discipline with an iron hand, was founded in 1811, and consists of about thirty Collegers and Oppidans, who jealously guard their special privileges of dress and conduct.

Eton always has, and probably always will, provoke endless criticism, but its present system of giving privacy and responsibility tends to produce real leaders in all walks of life, and no school has inspired a greater affection in its scholars. There is a vast library of reminiscences and descriptions by Etonians, ranging from the official History by Sir H. Maxwell-Lyte to the quaint little book *A Day of my Life, or Everyday Experiences at Eton* by 'An Eton Boy', published in 1877. Eton's poets, too, have given enchanting expression to their affection.

In June 1947 the College held its delayed Quincentenary Exhibition—and still the College carries on its great traditions. It is a record of endeavour and achievement so outstanding, and so redounding to England's credit, that all unbiased critics may well join with Etonians past and present in saying 'Floreat Etonia'.

CHAPTER TWO: *The Thames Bank: Boveney to Hedsor*

WEST of Windsor Bridge the river makes a long, lazy curve past the Eton boating-rafts and the Brocas, and skirts the fields of Eton Wick, with the College bathing-places, to Boveney Lock, giving a succession of magnificent views of Windsor Castle. Shortly after Boveney Lock is passed, a field path runs to the village of Boveney, past the small copse in which the quaint little church of Boveney is hidden. The tiny hamlet is dominated by picturesque Boveney Court, which dates in part from the seventeenth century.

North of Boveney is the wide Dorney Common, and the delightful village of Dorney, which, although it lies a mile or more away, has fields and woods reaching down to the Thames, and can be visited easily from the river. Dorney is a picturesque survival, with its mellow timber and brick houses, its historic manor-house, and its church. Dorney manor is mentioned in Domesday Book, and there are records which seem to point to the lords of the manor living there, but in its present form Dorney Court dates from the early Tudor period. The original fireplaces, panelling, and other fine fittings remain, with much beautiful contemporary furniture, and some interesting pictures.

The sixteenth-century owners of Dorney were the Hills, who had a life-long quarrel with Thomas Woodford of Britwell Manor, and their acrimonious correspondence is preserved. In 1531 Woodford wrote: 'Master Hyll, I am enfourmed that you have been oons or twyse at my grounds att Heggeley Hyll rydyng about the same with your tennants and varelets. If I fynde yowe after that maner ther ageyn I wyll make yow to goo a fote to Dorney or yt shall coste me my lyff.' Further accusations, acts of aggression and retaliation followed until the death of Richard Hill in 1540. His sons sold Dorney to William Garrard, afterwards Lord Mayor of London.

In 1624 the Palmers of Wingham, in Kent, bought Dorney from the Garrard family, and settled there, where they have remained to the present day. A Pedigree of the Palmer family, tracing their descent back to Charlemagne, is preserved at Dorney Court. The first Palmer to live at Dorney was a gentleman of the king's bedchamber and a chancellor of the Order of the Garter. He suffered greatly during the Civil War, his goods at Dorney being seized, and the house damaged by Parliamentary soldiers hoping to find money.

Sir James's eldest son by his second wife, born at Dorney Court in 1634, married Barbara Villiers, who afterwards became the mistress of Charles II. The King created him Earl of Castlemaine, but he was far from being a complaisant husband, and went abroad after a violent quarrel with his wife.

It was at Dorney that the first pineapple was grown in England, and a copy of a painting at Ham House is preserved at Dorney Court. It depicts Rose, the head gardener of Dorney, presenting a pineapple to Charles II at Hampton Court. The Pineapple Inn at Dorney, whose name always arouses the curiosity of visitors, commemorates the incident.

Dorney church is first mentioned about 1218, and its history shows that medieval people, although pious, were also distinctly grasping and quarrelsome at times—not excepting the priests themselves. There was a long-standing quarrel between the Lords of Dorney Manor and the Priors of Marlow for the advowson. It was alienated to Burnham Abbey in 1338, but towards the end of the century one of the lords of Dorney carried off the greater part of the tithes to his manor-house by force, and even took the carts and horses of the abbess!

Dorney church is an agreeable blending of twelfth-century

and Perpendicular work, with a seventeenth-century chapel and a considerable amount of excellent woodwork, including a musicians gallery. There is a splendid Jacobean monument to Sir William Garrard, with alabaster effigies showing him in armour, with Elizabeth, his wife, and the kneeling figures of seven sons and eight daughters, five of whom hold skulls.

Sir Thomas Palmer, and his son Philip, who was cup-bearer to Charles II, both of whom fought in the Civil War, were also buried in the church. Dorney was the birthplace of Richard Montagu, successively Bishop of Chichester and Norwich, and the friend of Laud, who described him as 'a very good scholar and a right honest man'. He wrote and published many famous works, his aim throughout his life being to support the Church of England against its enemies. Another native of Dorney was Robert Rave, one of the unfortunates who became martyrs for their faith.

ii

The lazy windings of the river between low-lying, willow-bordered banks continue until Maidenhead Bridge is reached, and then the Buckinghamshire bank rises in all the glory of tree-clad cliffs, to make one of the loveliest and most famous reaches of the Thames. Maidenhead Bridge was opened in 1777, a feast being held in honour of the occasion at a cost of £43 13s. 6d. Tolls were collected on the bridge until 1903. The handsome red-brick railway bridge was designed by Brunel, and its two main arches are said to be the widest brick arches in the world. The 'sounding arch' on the Buckinghamshire side is noted for its curious echo. It is the bridge painted by Turner for his picture *Rain, Steam and Speed*, now in the National Gallery.

The woods of Taplow and Cliveden, rising high above flood-level, naturally provided a refuge for Early Man, and important finds have been made in the neighbourhood. The river-bed near Taplow furnished some Bronze Age weapons of an unusually interesting character, including spear heads and swords. A bronze sickle found there has been described as by far the most important Bronze Age object yet found in the county. An Iron Age sword and a beautifully decorated scabbard were found at Amerden, a mile south of Taplow, and one of the best-preserved bowls of Neolithic 'B' culture was noticed by an angler, sticking out of the river-bank near Hedsor, a mile or so to the north. All the finds are now in the British Museum.

Taplow appears to have been a place of some importance in Anglo-Saxon days, for at Bapsey Pool, on the slope below Taplow Court overlooking the river, is traditionally the place where St. Birinus, first Bishop of Dorchester, baptised the earliest converts to Christianity in the district, about 1,300 years ago. Bapsey, a corruption of baptism, is found in the oldest records and maps of the district. Nearby is the site of the old church of Taplow, long since vanished. The land in front of Taplow Court is still known as Berry or Bury Fields, and quantities of pottery fragments dating from British, Roman, and Saxon times have been picked up on or near the surface of the old churchyard. More important still is the mound or barrow which still stands 30 yards from the west end of the old church. It yielded a wonderful hoard of Anglo-Saxon ornaments and weapons of gold and silver-gilt when excavated in 1883. The finds included a remarkable golden buckle set with garnets and lapis lazuli; a pair of beautifully ornamented clasps of gilt bronze; bronze and silver-gilt mounted drinking-horns, beautifully designed glass tumblers, and large buckets, all of which are now in the British Museum.

The older part of Taplow is clustered round the Victorian church, which fortunately preserves some interesting features from the original church, including some seventeenth-century panelling, and very fine brasses, some of which are palimpsests. There is a small effigy of a priest, Nichole de Aumberdene, dated 1350, within the head of a beautiful floriated cross, and the other brasses form a group of figures of the Manfeld family, who held the estate of Amerden in 1433. There is also a sixteenth-century brass to Thomas Jones and his wife Ursula, on which it is recorded she had been imprisoned for her faith. Taplow's royalist sympathizers seem to have been very courageous, for during the Commonwealth Dr. Edmunds remained in the parish, maintaining he was the true rector and no tithes ought to be paid to his successor. Although he was eventually compelled to promise conformity in 1647, Sir Thomas Hampson and one of the churchwardens still refused to recognize or pay the Puritan minister!

Only the turrets of Taplow Court can be seen above the trees from the river. Taplow Court was the seat of the Hampsons in the seventeenth century, and was partly rebuilt and enlarged by the Earl of Orkney in the eighteenth century. The present house is a Victorian mansion of the Desboroughs, haunted by the memory of the splendid receptions held there in the great days of the Victorian era, and with thoughts of those charming, ill-fated brothers, Julian and Billy Grenfell, sons of the first and last Lord Desborough. Athletes, sportsmen, and scholars, they were also poets of no mean ability, and might have made a great name for themselves had they not fallen in the flower of their youth during the 1914–18 war. Lord Desborough, the grandson of the original Grenfell at Taplow, was a great athlete in his day, and twice swam Niagara.

Above Boulters' Lock, once a veritable parade of fashion on Ascot Sunday, and still crowded throughout the boating season, the woods of Taplow merge into the still lovelier woodlands climbing the long ridge of hills on which Cliveden House is set, nearly 300 feet above the river.

The original house on the site, a magnificent palace built

by George Villiers, Duke of Buckingham, the favourite of
Charles II, was visited by John Evelyn in July, 1679, who
described it in his *Diary*.

It was to Cliveden that the Duke fled with the Countess of
Shrewsbury, who is said to have held her lover's horse whilst
he fought a duel with her husband, an event to which Pope
referred when he wrote of:

> 'Cliefden's proud alcove,
> The bower of wanton Shrewsbury and Love.'

The house was occupied for some time by Frederick,
Prince of Wales, the father of George III, during which time
James Thomson was a frequent visitor. In August, 1740, his
Alfred, a Mask of Liberty was presented in the grounds of
Cliveden for the entertainment of his princely host. Dr.
Arne composed the air of *Rule Britannia* especially for the
performance.

Cliveden was destroyed by fire in 1795, caused by a
servant reading in bed. Her candle caught the curtains, and
as she became insensible, she was unable to give the alarm
until the flames had spread too far. It was rebuilt in 1830,
from the design of John Shaw, but was again burned down
in 1849. The present house was built in 1851, from the
designs of Sir Charles Barry, who built the Houses of
Parliament.

The great brick terrace on which the house stands is the
original one built in 1666. It is about 450 feet long, and is
said to be on a level with the terrace at Windsor Castle.
There are many lodges, temples, and pavilions in the
grounds, the majority of which date from the eighteenth
century. The temples were designed by Giacomo Leoni, and
one was converted into a mausoleum to the first Viscount
Astor. The property was given to the National Trust by
Lord Astor, in 1942.

The lovely woods of Hedsor follow those of Cliveden,

and Hedsor House is also set on high ground, but can be seen best from above Cookham Lock. The house was built in 1862 on the site of an eighteenth-century mansion built by the second Lord Boston, and although picturesquely imitating a castle, is of no special interest. The church, on another hill in the park, is one of the smallest in the county. It was rebuilt in the nineteenth century, and only the arches and piers of the interior are left of the original medieval church, but its quaint belfry and its charming setting, no less than its enchanting views of the Thames and Wye, give it an attraction all its own. There is a tablet to Nathaniel Hooke, who is buried in the churchyard, together with his daughter. Hooke was the friend of Pope and many eminent men of letters, and was described by Dr. Johnson as 'a virtuous man, as his history shows'.

The charming Hedsor Wharf is a Victorian mansion incorporating a portion of an older house, and one of the mills on the little River Wye, which joins the Thames at Hedsor, is probably one of the two water-mills mentioned in 1492 and 1557. The remains of pile-dwellings of the Romano-British period were found near Hedsor Wharf, and when the 'New Cut' into Cookham Lock was made in 1830 some Roman swords and javelin heads, and human skeletons were found.

As it approaches Cookham Lock the river divides into four channels, two of which encircle Formosa Island, the largest island on the Thames.

CHAPTER THREE: *The Thames Bank: Bourne End to Fawley*

NO lock on the Thames has a lovelier situation than Cookham, which serves the enchanting Berkshire riverside resort of that name, and commands all the glorious Cliveden Reach. Farther upstream the high wooded cliffs sink once again to low-lying banks, with smooth lawns and fine riverside houses heralding the approach to Bourne End.

Bourne End is a purely modern resort which has grown up beside the long, straight reach which is one of the most popular on the river for yachting. The Upper Thames Sailing Club has its headquarters there, and the Sailing Week includes an open race for the Queen's Challenge Cup. The chief charm of Bourne End is in the delightful panorama it commands of the Berkshire bank of the river.

A mile or so upstream is the Spade Oak Ferry, where there is a path running inland to Little Marlow, with its attractive group of church, manor-house, inn, and old brick cottages.

Although portions of the church date from the twelfth century, there is a medley of all periods, but the majority of visitors in the present day are attracted more by the plain tombstone in the churchyard which marks the last resting-place of that curious and colourful personality, Edgar Wallace, one of the most prolific story-writers of any age, whose own life was more vivid and filled with incident than even the most eventful of his romances.

The neighbouring manor-house incorporates early seventeenth-century work, and Westhorpe House, beside the road to Great Marlow, dates from the reign of Queen Anne. During the eighteenth century it was successively occupied by Dr. Maddox, Bishop of Worcester, Everard Faulkener, Ambassador to the Porte and Postmaster-General, and General Nugent, who was M.P. for Buckingham for many years, and died there in 1849. A stream flowing eastward from Westhorpe House empties itself into the Thames near the site of Little Marlow Nunnery, which stands in the grounds of the modern Abbey House. It was small, and never very wealthy, and at the time of the Dissolution there were only two nuns and four servants. Excavations carried out in 1902 revealed practically the whole of the foundations of the nunnery.

It is two miles by road from Little to Great Marlow, but by far the most delightful way is to follow the towing-path, which gives a captivating panorama of the Berkshire bank, where the famous Quarry Woods rival those of Cliveden in beauty.

The Thames Valley is famous for the charm of its many small, historic towns, but none is more lovable than Great Marlow.

Marlow has been a place of considerable importance since the earliest times, and as early as 1294 an indulgence was granted for the repair of a bridge there. It has sent representatives to Parliament, and suffered during the troublous times of the Civil War, but now, in spite of its popularity with anglers and watermen, has a tranquillity all its own. Time has touched it very lightly, and there are a number of old and interesting houses surviving, but none attracting more attention than that in which Shelley settled after a visit to Thomas Love Peacock in 1816. Shelley wrote his poetry in a boat beside the beechwoods of Bisham, whilst his wife, Mary Wollstonecraft, to whom he dedicated it, wrote her strange masterpiece *Frankenstein* in the house which is now marked by a plaque, where they lived for the greater part of a year. Among their visitors were Godwin, Leigh Hunt, and other friends, but not Byron as the plaque suggests.

Beechwood, high above the river, is a Victorian mansion which has replaced the old house bought in 1863 by Frank Smedley, author of *Frank Fairlegh*, *Lewis Arundel*, and other novels which achieved a wide popularity in their day. He was a native of the town, and is buried there. George Payne Rainsford, the most prolific novelist of his day, also lived at Great Marlow for a time. Encouraged by both Scott and Washington Irving, he wrote over a hundred novels, chiefly on historical subjects. Yet another novelist, nearer our own time, and still a 'best seller', was Jerome K. Jerome, who lived at Marlow for many years, and described the town affectionately in his immortal *Three Men in a Boat*.

The Omar Khayyám Club, founded in 1892, often held their summer dinners at the Crown Hotel, Marlow, and among the members were George Gissing and Grant Allen.

Even these celebrities by no means exhaust the tale of Marlow's residents who have achieved fame in some walk of life, but the list is too long to give in its entirety. Only three others, each commemorated in the town, will be mentioned: Charles Frohman, one of the most popular and successful of theatrical showmen on both sides of the Atlantic, who was drowned in the *Lusitania* and is remembered by a fine drinking-fountain; John Richardson, a native of Marlow, and Sir Miles Hobart, who represented Marlow in Parliament in 1628. The former is buried in the churchyard and the latter in the church. Richardson, who was referred to by Gilbert in *Patience*, was born in the workhouse, about 1767, and amassed a large fortune as a strolling player and showman. He left instructions in his will that he was to be buried in Marlow churchyard in the same grave as a spotted boy who had proved an attraction twenty years previously. A picture still hanging in the vestry shows the black-and-white spotted boy, whose story is told by Lipscomb:

'Mr. Richardson . . . purchased the child here commemorated, then an infant, as it is said, for the price of 1000

guineas, for the purpose of exhibiting so curious a pheno-
menon to the public. Mr. Richardson proved a most
benevolent patron to this little orphan, whom he caused to
be baptised at Newington, in Surrey, and afterwards educated with the utmost tenderness, until his premature death
in 1812, at the age of about 8 years when he was buried in
the ch-yard here, and has a gravestone with a long inscription to his memory; while this painting preserves a faithful
likeness of this curious and wonderful being, and is a monument of Mr. Richardson's munificence and affection.'

The monument in the church to Sir Miles Hobart, dated
1632, has a delicate and spirited relief of an overturned
coach, commemorating his death in a coach accident on
Holborn Hill. Although over-restored, the church has a
graceful spire which is a river-side landmark, and retains
several other interesting monuments, including a tablet to
the Rev. Thomas Langley, author of the *History of the Desborough Hundred*, who died in 1801 at the age of thirty-two.

The Roman Catholic church, designed by the elder Pugin,
is a very attractive building, and is neighboured by the school
designed by the younger Pugin. It is famous for a relic of
undoubted antiquity, believed to be the embalmed hand of
St. James. Brought to England by the Empress Matilda, it
was given by Henry I to the abbey of Reading, where it
remained until the Dissolution, and was discovered there in
the seventeenth century, among the abbey ruins when the
foundations of the new gaol were being dug, and eventually
found its way to Marlow.

Yet, when all is said and done, it is the charm of the town
and its surroundings that attracts and holds the majority of
its visitors, who love to 'discover' its many interesting old
houses for themselves—and there is indeed a wealth of interest to be found there.

The reach above the Bridge to Temple Lock is the Marlow
Regatta course, beyond which is Hurleyford House, de-

signed by Sir Robert Taylor in 1756. Set at the foot of a
well-timbered park, and facing Hurley across the river, it has
a fine terrace which was a favourite promenade of Prince
Louis Napoleon when he paid the house a visit in 1846.

A mile north of the town is Seymour Court, on the site of
an old house practically destroyed in the Civil War. There
is a tradition that the earlier house was the birthplace of
Queen Jane Seymour, but it appears to have no foundation in
fact. A mile beyond Seymour Court is Widmere Farm, in a
remarkably fine situation, interesting for its dairy, which was
originally a chapel of the Hospitallers, dating from the early
thirteenth century.

Still farther upstream on the Buckinghamshire bank is the
modern mansion of Danesfield, which has the site of a
Roman encampment in its grounds. Three-quarters of a
mile west is the village of Medmenham, hidden from the
river, but well worth the short walk up a country lane to see
its gabled seventeenth-century houses and Norman church.
In spite of the addition of a few modern houses, they still
make an attractive group, backed by a cliff-like hill crowned
by a seventeenth-century farm. The Swan-Upping on the
Thames used to end with a dinner of the Swan-Uppers at
Medmenham.

The reach of the Thames between Marlow and Medmenham has always been a great haunt of swans, and Marlow
records show that numerous grants of their custody were
made by the Crown in the sixteenth century, but by the nineteenth century they were owned by the Crown and the
Dyers' and Vintners' City Livery Companies. They are still
marked annually by the Companies during the Swan-
Upping, in the first week in August, the Crown having been
astute enough to claim all swans without a mark.

Although Medmenham village is on a busy main road, it
has a restfully old-world atmosphere, as though trying to
dissociate itself from the dark stories which cling to the

remains of the Cistercian abbey beside the river. The monks led such blameless lives in the three and a half centuries of the Abbey's existence as a religious community that its history was uneventful, and at the time of the Dissolution it was so poor and inoffensive that even the King's Commissioners could find no fault, and reported '. . . monks there, two; and both desyren to go to Houses of Religion; Servants none; bells etc. worth £2 6s. 8d.: the house wholly in ruin; the value of the movable goods £1 3s. 8d.; Woods none; Debts none.'

All these centuries of pious living, however, are now over-shadowed by the provocative doings of less than twenty years. It was in 1745 that Sir Francis Dashwood of West Wycombe, later Lord le Despencer, founded his 'Knights of St. Francis of Wycombe', who held their meetings in the abbey of Medmenham, which had been so skilfully restored that it is now difficult to distinguish the original work. The secrecy which enfolded the clubs' aims and functions ex-tended even to designating its members with a pseudonym, and gave rise to the wildest speculation. Among the mem-bers and their guests, it is said, were Frederick, Prince of Wales, the Duke of Queensberry, John Wilkes, and others of the highest rank and fashion. The most improbable stories circulated in their own day, and the fact that there is no possibility of proving the truth of any assertion has not prevented the keenest speculation ever since.

A great-grandson of one of the original members pointed out that the real 'Hellfire Club' was founded by the Duke of Wharton early in the reign of George I, and that the name has been erroneously applied to the Medmenham Brother-hood, but the name has stuck, and as long as the 'Knights of St. Francis' are remembered, they will be called by that more picturesque and suggestive name.

About two miles upstream is Hambleden Lock, with a miniature archipelago linked to the Buckinghamshire bank by a series of bridges across the foaming weirs and lashers. The extremely picturesque village lies a mile north of the river, in a wooded valley beloved by ramblers, with the Georgian and Stuart red-brick houses typical of the Buckinghamshire style. The Old Rectory and the manor-house are especially striking. The church, though pleasant enough, has been too much restored to have great architectural interest, but boasts some elaborate and interesting monuments. There are brasses of the fifteenth, sixteenth, and seventeenth centuries, showing male and female figures in contemporary costume, and a tomb believed to be that of Henry, son of the second Lord Sandys, who died in 1555, with a long inscription. Among other monuments is an ornate Jacobean monument to Sir Cope Doyley and his wife, with an inscription by Francis Quarles, poet laureate to James I, who was Lady Doyley's brother:

'In spirit a Jael,
Rebecca in grace, in heart an Abigail;
In works a Dorcas, to the Church a Hannah,
And to her spouse, Susannah,
Prudently simple, providentially wary;
To the world a Martha, and to Heaven a Mary.'

There is a carved Norman tub font, and some fine early sixteenth-century panelling bearing the arms of Cardinal Wolsey, traditionally said to have formed part of the Cardinal's bedstead. In the churchyard are the graves of W. H. Smith, first Lord Hambleden, of bookstall fame; Major George Howson, who organized the British Legion Poppy Factory at Richmond, and the Kendrick Mausoleum, dating from the early eighteenth century, which was sketched by Horace Walpole for his *Journal of Visits to County Seats*.

Hambleden was the birthplace of St. Thomas de Cantelupe, who came of a noble and wealthy family, and was the intimate friend of Simon de Montfort, after whose death he was obliged to remain abroad for several years, as a result of the part he had played in the Barons' War. After his return to England he was consecrated Bishop of Hereford in 1275, and became the trusted adviser of Edward I. Shortly after his death miracles were worked at his shrine in Hereford Cathedral, and after several applications to the Pope, he was canonized in 1320, by which time his cult was second only to that of St. Thomas à Becket.

Lord Cardigan, born at Hambleden nearly 600 years later, became the darling of the public, as a result of his leadership of the Charge of the Light Brigade in the Crimea.

Shortly before the 1914–18 war, the remains of a Roman villa and other interesting relics were found. They are preserved in a small museum.

In addition to the manor-house, is Yewden Manor, at the south end of the parish, which has in its grounds an avenue of yews of immense age. Greenlands, a short distance above the locks, and clearly visible from the river in its setting of colourful flower-beds, is an enormous Victorian mansion built by Lord Hambleden, close to the site of the original house garrisoned for the King in 1644. When the house 'could no longer be defended, the whole structure being beaten down by the cannon', Colonel Hawkins and his troops marched out with all the honours of war.

The long bend of the river at Greenlands ends in the famous Regatta Course to Henley Bridge, heralded by Regatta or Temple Island, beyond which Fawley Court, in its beautifully planted grounds, marks the county boundary between Buckinghamshire and Oxfordshire and the close proximity of Henley, just over the border.

Fawley Court occupies the site of the manor-house which was the home of Sir James Whitelocke, one of the Judges of the King's Bench, and his son, Bulstrode Whitelocke, author of the entertaining *Memorials of British Affairs*, and of the *Journal of the Swedish Embassy*, in which he gives a fascinating insight into life at the court of Queen Christina of Sweden when he was Ambassador there. The building was so badly damaged by the Royalists that it was eventually pulled down, and the present house built from designs by Sir Christopher Wren. Additions were made in the Victorian era in the same style, but the greater part remains unaltered, with magnificent interior decoration, including elaborate plaster-work, Chinese wallpaper, a white marble fireplace of Adam design, and other examples of the Adam style at its best.

The elaborate garden ornaments include a classic river gateway and a folly, an ornamental canal from the river to the house, and a dairy with a re-set Norman doorway from a vanished chapel at Henley, and another doorway brought from the Great Chamber in Crosby Hall, London.

Fawley village stands on a ridge some two miles north, on beech and yew-clad slopes of the Chilterns, and has several groups of seventeenth-century cottages, and two farms of the same date. The flint church has been rather over-restored, but the pulpit, lectern, wainscoting, and some carving by Grinling Gibbons remain, and there is a Jacobean monument to Sir James and Lady Whitelocke with alabaster effigies, and a fourteenth-century brass with a French inscription to a former rector.

CHAPTER FOUR: Slough: Old and New

IT is impossible to deny that Slough shows its least attractive face to those who speed along the Bath Road, and many hard things have been said about its modern development. Only to those who know it well does it reveal the charm and history of the little village from which the largest town of Buckinghamshire has sprung.

The phenomenal increase in the population of the town dates from the years between the two great world wars, and was the direct outcome of a decision by General Smuts, who arranged to send the motor-transport brought back from France after the 1914–18 war to the great depot created at Slough. Within a quarter of a century the 'Dump' became an important Trading Estate, drawing so many workers from all parts of the Kingdom that the vast increase in population transformed the little country town into a Borough, and necessitated a change in the parliamentary representation which gave the town its own Member of Parliament.

The majority of the 50,000 or 60,000 newcomers regard Slough as an entirely modern development, and would be astonished to hear that as long ago as the eighteenth century the great French astronomer Arago, paying tribute to W. Herschel, wrote: 'Slough is the place in the world where most discoveries have been made. The name of this village will never perish.' Still less do they realize that Slough was in existence as early as the thirteenth century, when the name was spent 'Slo', and that the modern spelling was first recorded between 1443 and 1444, in the accounts of Eton College, which was built from bricks made in a kiln set up at Slough in April 1442.

The introduction of coaches, in the reign of Elizabeth, and the subsequent development of Slough as a coaching centre, began a colourful train of events which culminated in the brilliant Georgian period, when many celebrities, and even royalties, were numbered among Slough's visitors. There were several fine coaching inns by the early seventeenth century, and by the reign of William IV between sixty and eighty coaches passed through Slough daily, over 1,000 horses being stabled in the coaching inns for their use.

William Herschel and his sister Caroline settled at Slough in 1786, shortly after his appointment as Private Astronomer to George III, which was the direct result of his discovery of the planet Uranus. It was the first time a planet had been discovered during the ages of recorded history, for all the five known before can be detected by the naked eye. The discovery was made whilst he was organist of the Octagon Chapel at Bath, and an entry in Caroline Herschel's diary makes curious reading in the present day, for she complains that the first time she went to market in Datchet—where they lived for a short time before settling at Slough—she was 'astonished at the dearness of every article . . . for at Bath I had the week before bought from 16 to 20 eggs for 6d, here I could get no more than five for 4d'.

Directly the Herschels moved into Observatory House at Slough, which is still in existence and inhabited by Sir William's descendants, he set up his 20-foot telescope on the lawn, and also worked unceasingly at his project for a giant 40-foot telescope. Many famous people, including George III, called to see it and walked through the tube, before the optical parts were finished.

Fanny Burney, whose father was a friend of William Herschel, records in her diary: 'By invitation of Mr. Herschel, I now took a walk which will sound to you rather strange: it was through his telescope! and it held me quite upright, and without the least inconvenience; so would it have done had I been dressed in feathers and a bell hoop— such is its circumference'.

The telescope was in use until 1815, or later. The tube was 39 feet 4 inches long, and the mirror, with a diameter of 49½ inches, weighed 2,118 lb. A section still remains in the garden, and the huge mirror hangs in the hall of the house. The telescope was for many years marked on the Ordnance Survey maps of the district as a landmark.

In addition to the giant telescope, Dr. Herschel made innumerable smaller instruments, which were in great demand all over Europe. The Empress Catherine of Russia bought many of his mirrors, and the King of Spain paid £3,150 for one of his telescopes. His fame became so widespread that his house at Slough became a place of pilgrimage for all the scientists of Europe, and among notabilities who came to pay their respects to the famous astronomer were the Archbishop of Canterbury, the Dukes of Kent, Sussex and Cambridge, Prince Galitzin, the Prince of Orange, Lord Palmerston, Maria Edgeworth, the novelist, and many others.

The King of Poland awarded him a gold medal, and all the great academies and scientific societies of Europe showered honours on him. He was created a Knight of the Royal Hanoverian Guelphic Order in 1816, and was the first President of the Astronomical Society, founded in 1821. In addition to this world-wide fame as an astronomer, Sir William invented a method of sequences which gave rise to Stellar photometry, and his discovery of 'infra-red' solar rays rendered possible the marvellous photographic effects of an infra-red camera.

Professor Holden said of him, 'As a practical astronomer, he remains without an equal. In profound philosophy he has few superiors. His is one of the few names which belong to the whole world.' Yet all who knew him paid tribute to his unassuming charm. He not only had the power to inspire a deep devotion in those most closely associated with him, but was himself of an extremely affectionate and faithful nature.

His sister Caroline was completely devoted to his interests, and a most selfless assistant in his work. Although she only took up the study of astronomy on her beloved brother's account, she later achieved no small success, discovering eight comets, five of them with undisputed priority, between 1786 and 1797. She was the first woman known to have made such discoveries. She was elected an honorary member of numerous scientific societies, and received the gold medal of the Astronomical Society in 1828.

Sir John Herschel, the only son of Sir William, was born at Observatory House in 1792, and achieved even greater fame than his father and aunt. He was described as 'a prodigy of science' when only seventeen, and was elected a Fellow of the Royal Society at the age of twenty-one, and captured many important scientific prizes. He added great scientific attainments to his astronomical studies, and his many important discoveries included that of hyposulphurous acid and its salts, which are invaluable in photography. All three of his sons were distinguished astronomers and scientists, and one of his descendants, another Sir William Herschel, first used the finger-print system for the identification of criminals whilst in the Bengal police, from whence it was introduced at Scotland Yard.

All the Slough inns had a prosperous time in the eighteenth century. They were frequented by many distinguished travellers, and figure in innumerable memoirs of the time. They were also a haunt of highwaymen, including 'Flying Hawkes', one of the most celebrated highwaymen of George III's reign, who terrorized the district for years.

The chief occupation of the villagers was agriculture and brick-making, and it is said that the Red Lion Inn, which stood opposite the Crown, was a haunt of the brick-makers, who, when work became slack between seasons, repaired there, 'remaining day and night on week-days and Sundays alike'—a state of affairs which might well arouse envy in these days of licensing restrictions and shortages! It was at the blacksmith's forge which then stood opposite the Red Lion that a quaint incident, recorded in Sir John Herschel's diary, took place. After Samuel Richardson's novel *Pamela* was published in 1740, the blacksmith, who was one of the few villagers who could read, used to read the fortnightly parts aloud as they appeared. The villagers followed the adventures of the heroine with such intense interest that when her difficulties ended in marriage they rushed off to the vicar of Upton and asked to ring the church bells in celebration!

Several of the most attractive of Slough's old inns have completely disappeared or been rebuilt since the beginning of the century. Of these, the Crown Hotel occupies the oldest site, for there has been an inn there since the fourteenth century at least. The Duke of Wellington twice stayed there, and Prince Albert spent the night there before the visit to Windsor Castle during which Queen Victoria proposed to him.

Apart from Observatory House, Slough's chief links with the past are so tucked away they must be specially sought. Oldest of all the surviving buildings is the original parish church of Upton-cum-Chalvey. Domesday Book records that the manor of Upton was held by King Harold and came to William the Conqueror at the Conquest. It was granted to Hugh de Beauchamp, and his son bestowed it upon the Priory of Merton in Surrey, in whose ownership it remained until the Dissolution. After passing through various hands, it came into the possession of Edward Lascelles, an ancestor of the present Earl of Harewood, in 1711, and remained in the family until 1926, during which time George Augustus

Sala, one of the founders of the Savage Club, and a popular journalist of his day, was one of the tenants. On 12 June 1886 Sala wrote in the *Illustrated London News*: 'I resided five and twenty years ago in a dear old house called Upton Court —a weird and ancient mansion, with high-pitched thatched roof and dormer windows, a very antique manor-house of the Tudor period, I should say, with a lake in front, and a garden all run to exquisitely picturesque wildness: and a rosery with eighteen varieties of roses, and a ghost, who, in consequence of her services in frightening servant-maids out of their wits, had been retained in the establishment for upwards of three hundred years.'

Sir Douglas Forsyth, the famous traveller in Central Asia, and Administrator in India, was a later tenant, and it was probably he who converted the lake into a sunken garden. The thatched roof has given place to tiles, but otherwise the old house remains as picturesque as ever. Built in the late fifteenth century, it was altered and enlarged in the seventeenth century, and has some contemporary oak panelling and inscriptions in the interior.

It is closely neighboured by Upton church, which is believed to mark the site of a Saxon foundation, and has a Norman doorway and other Norman work in the interior. There are some interesting brasses to the Bulstrode family, and a brass with a Hebrew inscription, which is a rarity. There is also a beautiful, though mutilated, alabaster representation of the Trinity, said to be of fifteenth-century Italian workmanship; a thirteenth-century carved oak arch, which is an elaborate example of woodwork of an unusually early date; and tablets to the memory of Sir William Herschel and other members of the family, who are buried in the church.

In the churchyard are a number of quaint epitaphs, including the often-quoted inscription to Sara Bramstone, a Jacobite lady who 'dared to be just in the reign of George II'.

The River Thames at Marlow

The Eton Montem, Salt Hill, in 1838

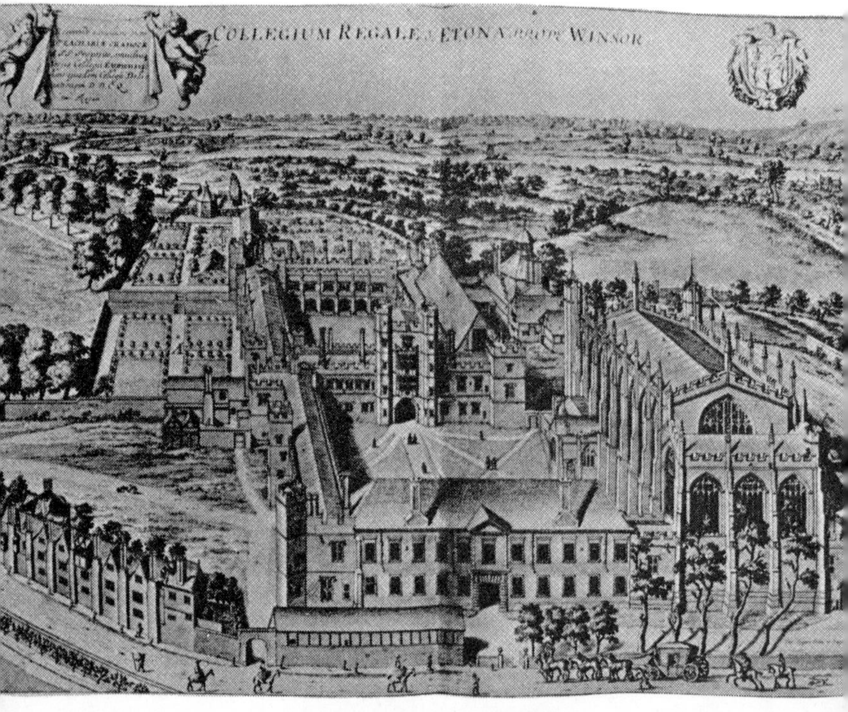

COLLEGIUM REGALE ETONA PROPE WINSOR

Eton College in 1688

George Fordham, the famous jockey, on whose tombstone is inscribed, 'It's the pace that kills'; Edward Matthew Ward, the Royal Academician, who painted many of his most famous pictures at Slough; and Richard Bentley, last head of the firm which published *Bentley's Miscellany* and its successor, *The Temple Bar Magazine*, and the novels of Dickens, Disraeli, Harrison Ainsworth, and other celebrated writers, are also buried at Upton.

There are some old houses in Upton, much altered, near the half-timbered Red Cow Inn, which is the very picture of what a country pub should be, with its setting of trees and flowers.

Chalvey has a small Victorian church designed by G. E. Street. The earliest known mention of Chalvey is in 1252. It was famous for its Eye Well in the eighteenth century, and both Queen Anne and Queen Charlotte bathed their eyes in its waters, which were taken to Windsor Castle daily, in buckets.

The present parish church of Slough, St. Mary's, was consecrated in 1837. Alfred Blanchett, one of a noted Slough family of musicians, who succeeded his father as organist of St. Mary's, composed the tune of *Souls of Men* and other well-known hymns. P. H. Eliot, who was rector from 1897 to 1921, and afterwards Bishop of Buckingham, is buried in the churchyard.

Hidden away in the heart of Slough is the beautiful seventeenth-century Baylis House, built for Dr. Godolphin, Provost of Eton and Dean of St. Paul's Cathedral, whose family crest of a dolphin can still be seen on the wrought-iron gates. Among later occupants of the house were Mary, Marchioness of Thomond, niece and heiress of Sir Joshua Reynolds, and ward of Edmund Burke; and the Lord Chesterfield who wrote the famous *Letters* to his son. In 1830 it became a Roman Catholic school—one of the first established after the Catholic Emancipation Act. Among its pupils were Cardinal Merry del Val, Archbishop Butt, and Sir Seymour Hicks. The school was given up after it had celebrated its centenary, and the house now belongs to the Borough Council.

Another famous school in Slough was run at Aldin House by the father of the late Charles Hawtrey, the actor, during which time it had a number of pupils who later became famous, including the first Earl Baldwin.

Slough has been extremely important horticulturally. Browns' Nurseries, founded some time in the eighteenth century, introduced the *Lilium Brownii*, said to have bloomed first in England in 1837. Charles Turner, who took over Browns', was even more famous. Dean Hole in his *Book of Roses* called him the 'King of Rose-growers' for the exceptional number of new varieties he introduced, which included the Crimson Rambler. The equally popular Mrs. Sinkins Pink was raised by the Matron of the Workhouse in Slough.

The coming of the railway naturally made an immense difference to Slough. In August 1838, only two months after the opening of the line, the many famous coaches began to come off the roads, and turnpike tolls fell from £18 to £4 a week. Slough station was used frequently by Prince Albert, Queen Victoria, and their guests. On one occasion the Empress of Austria, when delayed by a snowstorm, was wheeled with her ladies across the sloppy platform on luggage trolleys, regaled with cold beef in the Royal Saloon, and borrowed the *Ingoldsby Legends* from the station-master, to pass away the time.

The first electric telegraph in the world was installed between Slough and Paddington in 1843, and a message sent by it on New Year's Day, 1845, resulted in the arrest of John Tawell, who murdered a woman at Salt Hill and escaped by train to London, where he was met by detectives— the first murderer ever arrested by this means.

ii

Although the Montem Mound was within the boundaries of the old parish of Upton-cum-Chalvey, the Salt Hill Inns, with which the ceremony was so closely associated, were just across the Chalvey Brook, which marked the western boundary. The origin of 'Montem' is obscure, but the earliest known account was compiled by William Malim, Headmaster of Eton, about 1560. He described it as an initiation of new boys at Salt Hill by sprinkling them with 'sal' in its double meanings of 'salt' and 'wit'. By the eighteenth century it had become a sham military march, and was then frankly a festival for the purpose of collecting 'salt'-money contributions towards the expense of the Senior Colleger when he went to King's College, Cambridge. By 1712 the salt was given not to the boys, but to the passers-by, who were made to pay for it. The salt was collected by two 'salt-bearers' assisted by ten or twelve 'runners' or 'servitors', all dressed in fancy costumes, who scoured all the approaches to Eton and Windsor, carrying staves and satin money-bags emblazoned with the college arms. A pinch of salt was given to the donor of money, and a little blue ticket inscribed with a motto, which the recipient put in his hat, or otherwise displayed prominently as protection from further demands for the rest of the day—surely the first known flag-days?

In its later phases the whole school mustered in semimilitary array and attire, and marched in procession to the Montem Mound, two miles away. Doggerel rhymes were composed for the occasion and sold to the spectators.

The average amount collected latterly was £1,000, but this was subject to deductions for the payment of expenses, including a breakfast to all the sixth- and fifth-form boys, and a dinner afterwards to friends, and the captain seldom received more than half the proceeds—and if he was unpopular a bill for damages was deliberately run up to still further reduce the amount.

In 1847 Dr. Hawtrey, after much hesitation, decided to abolish the custom, as the opening of the railway had attracted great crowds of undesirable sightseers from London.

The two inns most closely associated with the Eton Montem were the Castle and Botham's Windmill Inn. The former has been reconstructed as the Salt Hill Hotel, and the latter is only remembered in the name of another hotel on a neighbouring site. It was at the Castle Inn that a dinner was given to the Commissioners of the Colnbrook Turnpike Trust in 1773, when all but one of the twenty died as the result of taking soup from a copper pan which had formed verdigris. The unfortunate inn-keeper died of vexation shortly afterwards.

Botham's Windmill Hotel was a great centre for sportsmen, and Hunt dinners were held there by the Berkeley Hunt and by the Royal Buckhounds. The list of distinguished visitors to Botham's is almost endless, but its most distinguished gathering was in June, 1814, when the Prince Regent entertained the Emperor of Russia, the King of Prussia, and his sons (both of whom afterwards became Kings of Prussia, and the younger, later, Emperor of Germany), the Prince of Orange, the Grand Duke of Oldenburg, and other notabilities.

Fourteen years later Salt Hill had another notable occasion when a special meet of the King's Buckhounds was held there in honour of Don Miguel of Portugal. Don Miguel, who was accompanied by the Master of the Staghounds, who was a brother of the famous Duke of Wellington, was habited in English hunting costume and rode a beautiful black horse from the King's stud. About 200 gentlemen joined the hunt, including the Duke of Devonshire, Lords Mountcharles, Strathaven, Kinnaird and Berkeley, General Grosvenor, and several foreign noblemen—so it is fortunate that 'good sport was had in a thirty-five minutes hard run'.

iii

Since the extension of the Borough other interesting and historic sites have been brought within the Slough boundaries, including Cippenham, where the site of the old palace of the Saxon kings of England can still be very clearly seen, although nothing whatever remains of the palace. There are numerous references in their household accounts to visits of the Saxon kings to Cippenham, and it was also used on occasion by the Norman kings, but its most colourful owner was Richard, Earl of Cornwall, and King of the Romans, whose charter for the foundation of Burnham Abbey was dated at Cippenham. Excitement must have been intense on the great day in 1266 when he and his brother, Henry III, and a magnificent array of bishops and barons, gathered at Cippenham to witness the founding of the abbey.

After the death of Richard's son and heir, Edmund, Cippenham passed through many hands, but there is no record to show whether any of the owners ever lived there, or when the manor-house fell into disuse.

In the present day, behind the pre-fabs and council houses which Cippenham shows to the passer-by, the old village lingers on with some interesting old houses round the village green, which escaped the Enclosure Acts and is safeguarded by a special clause, inserted when Cippenham was transferred to Slough, maintaining the right of the villagers to graze their geese and other animals on the green.

An early eighteenth-century house in Cippenham Lane was once the home of Jacob Bryant, a scholar who was celebrated in his day. George III spent hours gossiping with him. In his youth Bryant was first tutor and afterwards secretary to the Duke of Marlborough, who gave him rooms at Blenheim Palace, and allowed him the use of the library, where he occupied himself with antiquarian research. One of his friends said he 'knew everything up to Noah, and nothing after the deluge'. He was buried at Farnham Royal, beneath the seat he had occupied in the church.

iv

On the east, the extension of Slough brought much of Langley within the borough.

Langley Marish parish church, flanked by two rows of seventeenth-century almshouses, and neighboured by a picturesque old inn, makes a charming picture, and the church itself is of exceptional interest. Part of the building dates from the twelfth century, but a unique feature is the Kedermister Pew and Library, which were added in the seventeenth century by Sir John Kedermister, Lord of the Manor, as his private pew.

The pew has latticed panels, through which the occupiers can see the whole church, without themselves being seen. A wide-open eye—the 'eye of God'—is repeated over and over again in small panels, and another curious feature is the design of the cushions which cover the seats, showing the head, many times repeated, of the Duke of Marlborough, who owned Langley Park in the eighteenth century. The library opens out from the pew. It is wainscoted and painted with a variety of designs, including the arms of the Keder-misters and their alliances, views of Windsor Castle and Eton College, portraits of Sir John Kedermister and his wife, and figures of saints. There is a great seventeenth-century fire-place, with an overmantel elaborately decorated with painted figures and arabesques, and a contemporary table. The books are contained in wainscot presses, fitted with doors painted to match the rest of the wainscoting.

Amongst the books was an eleventh-century copy of the Gospels, and other valuable books now in the British Museum for safe keeping. A framed catalogue on vellum, dated 1638, hangs in the library. The *Pharmacopolium*, or *Medecine book of John and Mary Kedermister* dated 1630, now in Aylesbury Museum, contains many quaint recipes, including one 'for a medicine to comfort the heart' which reads: 'Take a quantity of good ale and a handful of bayleaves, and a spoonful of graines, seethe all together, straine and put a little sugar thereunto, and drinke it evening and morning and it will comfort and strengthen the hearte very much'. Graines, incidentally, are now known as cardamom seed.

There is a tradition that Milton used the library whilst living at Horton.

There are some elaborate mural tablets and monuments in the church, and a fine Jacobean pulpit. Among those buried in the vault below the church are Ursula, Marchioness of Normanby, Lady Palmiston, Sir John Kedermister and various members of the family, whose coffins can be seen by the curious through a small open grating on the outside wall of the church.

Although Langley Park and Black Park are outside Slough, the Borough Council are joint owners with the Eton Rural District and the County Council, in an endeavour to preserve these beautiful estates as part of the Green Belt.

The estate at Langley was bought by the third Duke of Marlborough in 1738. He pulled down the old manor-house of the Kedermisters, with the exception of the orangery and the enormous range of stables, and built the present mansion. The grounds, with their wonderful array of rare trees and flowering shrubs, were laid out by the fourth Duke, who later sold the park to Robert Harvey, in whose family it remained until acquired by the local authorities in 1944.

The adjoining Black Park, which was planted out about the middle of the seventeenth century, is now a completely natural woodland, chiefly of fir and pine, and is especially beautiful in the neighbourhood of the small lake.

Ditton Park, which lies just outside the Slough boundary, to the south of Langley, has known a number of distinguished owners. There is a tradition that Queen Elizabeth, when Princess, spent part of her girlhood there. The original house was built by Sir John Molins, of Stoke Poges. It was rebuilt by Sir Ralph Winwood, Secretary of State to James I, who appointed him Keeper of the Messuage and Park of Ditton, where he built a mansion on the site of the medieval building. This house was destroyed by fire in 1812, and was replaced by the present mansion, built in the following year from the designs of a pupil of James Wyatt. The old moat and drawbridge were retained, and give it a picturesque appearance. It is now the Admiralty Compass Observatory.

CHAPTER FIVE: *In and Around Burnham Beeches*

THE glory of Buckinghamshire is its great beech-woods, which once covered the whole area with dense forest, and still beautify the Chiltern Country. None are lovelier than those of Burnham Beeches, which were bought by the Corporation of the City of London in 1878, as a public playground.

Burnham Beeches was never a forest in the strict sense of the word, even in Norman times. To-day it consists of about 300 acres of woodland and an area of open land now known as East Burnham Common. There are about 800 beech-trees whose grotesque shape is due to continuous pollarding to provide firewood for the lord of the manor and his tenants, which was not discontinued until about 1820. Since that date the shoots have grown up into the great branch systems that are such a unique feature of the woodland to-day. The tradition that they were pollarded by Cromwell's soldiers may also be true, as some of them were stationed at the neighbouring village of Burnham in December 1645— and doubtless took steps to provide themselves with fires!

The name of Egypt, an area of common where there are fine silver birches, and the adjoining Egypt Woods, invariably excite curiosity, but as the name was not in use until after the middle of the sixteenth century, it is most probably a corruption of 'Egyptians', the early name for gypsies, who camped there.

Seven Ways Plain marks the site of an old British encampment—possibly used by the British chief, Caedwalla, who was living in the forest of the Chilterns in A.D. 685. There is also a Saxon homestead moat known as Harlequin's or Hardicanute's moat, surrounded by a hedge and ditch enclosing about twenty acres.

It is the never-failing, ever-changing beauty of the woodlands themselves which is the supreme attraction of Burnham Beeches, whether in spring, with the yellow-green buds unfolding above a carpet of bluebells; in early summer, when the massed purple of the rhododendrons makes a glorious splash of colour against the satiny-grey beech-trunks; in autumn, when the trees themselves are afire with gold, copper and red against the glistening green of holly trees, or in winter, when the strange and often beautiful contours of the trees can be seen to best advantage. No wonder there are happy crowds there on every fine week-end—but nothing can mar the perfection of these woods, with their miniature hills and valleys, and it is always possible to penetrate sufficiently far into their more remote fastnesses, where crowds never find their way even at week-ends, whilst during the week the beauty-lover can have an almost perfect solitude.

Strangely enough, for all their incomparable charm and the number of poets who lived in the neighbourhood, the Beeches have figured but little in literature. Gray refers to them once or twice in his letters, but never seems to have been inspired to describe them, apart from a humorous reference to them as 'very reverend vegetables'. Only two lesser poets have been moved to verse: the Rev. J. Mitford, editor of the first accurate edition of the *Poems of Thomas Gray*, has some indifferent poetry on the subject, and Henry Luttrell, the poet and wit who was in the Holland House set, wrote:

'Over many a dell and upland walk,
    Their sylvan beauty reaches.
Of Birnam Wood let Scotland boast,
    While we've our Burnham Beeches.'

Dorneywood, a modern house in 250 acres of ground, on the west of Burnham Beeches, has been given to the Nation by Lord Courtauld-Thomson, as a future official residence for a Cabinet Minister.

ii

Two miles south of Burnham Beeches is the village of Burnham, which was formerly a place of considerable importance, particularly after the foundation of Burnham Abbey, when a weekly market and yearly fair were held. Until comparatively recent times the main road to the west ran considerably to the north of the present road after leaving Salt Hill, and Burnham was at an important cross-roads. Nevertheless, it had a placidly prosperous existence untouched by any outstanding events. Although so near London, it does not seem to have seen any fighting in the Civil War, when Parliamentarians were quartered there— but there must have been a tremendous local scandal in 1645, when Lieutenant Ryder and 'divers others of his troopers (were) found typpling in a very deboyce manner' and refused to pursue a party of Royalist horse from Oxford, who had carried off two men and weapons from Cippenham.

Burnham church was altered and enlarged about the time that Burnham Abbey was built, and has fourteenth-century and fifteenth-century additions, which have made it the largest flint church in the county. It is fortunate in possessing sixteen ancient deeds ranging in date from 1296 to 1400, which give interesting details of local properties. The inscriptions 'The Pope is a Vilin' and 'The Pope is a knave' cut on one of the pillars of the south aisle probably date from the eighteenth century.

There are some excellent examples of sixteenth-century brasses to the memory of the Eyre family of Allards, of three generations, one of which has an acrostic inscription, dated 1581. A white marble monument to Mr. Justice Willes, who died in 1787, has a medallion of the judge in profile, carved by John Bacon, who won the first medal awarded by the

Royal Academy for sculpture. A delightful portrait bust commemorates Vicar Wright, who was vicar of Burnham from 1560 to 1594, and among numerous others of more or less interest buried in the church are George Evelyn, uncle of the diarist, Jonathan Rogers, the uncle with whom Gray stayed at Cant's Hill, now known as Burnham Grove, Lord Grenville of Dropmore, and Samuel Christie Miller.

Gray gives a brief but vivid description of his uncle's household in a letter dated September 1737: '. . . I arrived safe at my uncle's, who is a great hunter in imagination; his dogs take up every chair in the house, so I am forced to stand at this present writing; and though the gout forbids him galloping after them in the field, yet he continues still to regale his ears and nose with their comfortable noise and stink. He holds me mighty cheap, I perceive, for walking when I should ride, and reading when I should hunt. . . .'

Samuel Christie Miller inherited and added to the famous library at Britwell House, which included fine specimens of early English and Scottish literature. When the library was sold in 1919, one small volume alone containing the original and only known copy of Shakespeare's *Venus and Adonis* fetched £15,100, the highest sum ever paid at an auction for a printed book or manuscript.

Britwell House was originally known as Britwell Court, and among various owners was Charles Boyle, Earl of Orrery, of astronomical fame. The house is now occupied by an Anglican religious community. Nashdom, built by Sir Edwin Lutyens for Prince Alexis Dolgorouki, is now a Benedictine monastery.

Burnham Abbey, which lies a mile and a half south of the village, has been restored, and is to-day occupied by the Society of the Precious Blood, an Anglican community which follows the rule of St. Augustine, as did the original foundation, and which took possession on the 18th April,

1916, the six hundred and fiftieth anniversary of the signing of the foundation charter.

After the brilliant gathering which signalized its original foundation, Burnham Abbey had little or no history until the last real Abbess, Margaret Gibson, refused to acknowledge the supremacy of Henry VIII, and was superseded by Alice Baldwin, who meekly signed the deed of surrender.

Although the church has practically gone, there are extensive remains of the cloister buildings, dating from the thirteenth century. Unfortunately, as the Order now occupying the abbey is strictly enclosed, it is not possible to examine the buildings. The Chantry House next door to the abbey is Tudor, and just beyond is the old tithe barn, dating from 1265, which has been restored and turned into a dwelling-house.

Just across the Dorney road from Burnham Abbey is Huntercombe Manor in its beautiful gardens. Built originally in the fourteenth century, it consisted of the present hall, with a west wing, now much altered, and an east wing rebuilt and enlarged about 1705. A good deal of the original work remains internally, and there are some fine panelled rooms and a staircase of sixteenth-century work.

A sixteenth-century owner of Huntercombe was Paul Wentworth, who seems to have embodied all the more disagreeable 'virtues'. He is usually credited with the introduction of prayers in Parliament, but actually carried a motion to add a sermon of an hour and a half in addition to prayers. In 1589, in a letter to the Queen asking for a further lease of Burnham Abbey, he reminded her that she had shown her confidence in him by committing to his charge at his house at Burnham 'the late Duke of Norfolk'. A note at the foot of the letter shows that the Queen replied favourably: 'Her majesty most princely calling to mind the long and dutiful service of this suppliant, her highness's servant, his loyal care, trouble and charge at the committing of the late Duke of Norfolk to his house'.

In the following century George Evelyn, uncle of the diarist, owned Huntercombe, and was succeeded by his son, also George. In August 1679 John paid a visit to his cousin, and described the house in his *Diary*.

The house was afterwards continually let on lease until bought by the Hon. Richard Boyle, whose wife created a perfect garden, wrote a number of delightful books and articles signed E.V.B., which are still much sought after by garden lovers, and raised a variety of new species of flowers.

Her best-known works were *Days and Hours in a Garden*, which describes a year's work in the garden of Huntercombe, and *Seven Gardens and a Palace*, in which she gives a charming description of the house and manor, and recalls that Jane Porter had described it seventy years earlier in *Tales Round a Winter Hearth*, having planned the story whilst living in the house. The beautiful *Viola gracilis Huntercombe Purple* is one of the plants Mrs. Boyle first raised at Huntercombe Manor.

A fine ironwork grille in the garden wall of Huntercombe was removed to the Garden Terrace at Dropmore, which lies six miles north of Huntercombe, by Lord Grenville, who was Pitt's Foreign Secretary from 1791 to 1801, and head of the 'Ministry of All the Talents', formed on the death of Pitt in 1806. He owned both estates, but lavished all his affection on Dropmore, which he built and beautified himself. This part of Burnham was a wild common when he bought it in 1792 and began to realize his boyhood dream of laying out a superb park and gardens. It has been said that the view from one of the terraces of Dropmore inspired Thomas Gray to write his *Ode on a Distant Prospect of Eton College*. Rogers, the banker-poet, Nichol, and Lord Stratford de Redcliffe, also commemorated their visits in verse. The gardens were laid out with matchless skill and taste. Lord Grenville brought trees and flowering shrubs from all parts of the world to grace the 600 acres of grounds, including one of the first wistarias raised in England.

South of Dropmore is Hitcham, reached by shady lanes so long and winding that it seems remote from the modern world.

Hitcham church has a Norman nave, a fourteenth-century chancel, with splendid Jacobean woodwork, and retains much of its original stained glass, dating back to 1340, and some encaustic tiles, on which are shown a mermaid, a hound hunting a stag, and a horseman with a falcon. There are also some sixteenth-century brasses, and an elaborate monument to Sir William Clarke, who entertained Queen Elizabeth at the now vanished Hitcham manor-house in 1602.

Dr. John Friend, the noted physician, who was one of the remarkable group of men numbered among the friends of Harley and Bolingbroke in the reign of Queen Anne, is described as lord of the manor on a slab recording his death in 1728. In the churchyard is a memorial to Princess Dolgorouki.

The remains of the old manor-house where Queen Elizabeth was entertained consist only of walls of seventeenth-century brick, which once enclosed the kitchen gardens, and the wrought-iron gates. Thomas Garrard of Dorney, who married Dorothy, daughter of Sir William Clarke, against his father's wish, had cause to regret his disobedience, for his father-in-law and wife combined to thrust him out of his inheritance, called him rogue and rascal, and refused to admit him into their house, his wife sending him a message 'that if he lay in the streets and starved, he should not have a groat for his releife of her', and he had to bring an action to recover his estate.

Among several interesting old houses surviving in the parish is Hitchambury, which was formerly the rectory, and Hitcham Farm, an early seventeenth-century house, much altered.

The road running east from Burnham to Farnham Royal

passes East Burnham Park. Richard Sheridan and his bride,
Elizabeth Linley, spent their honeymoon at East Burnham
Cottage. In 1838 George Grote settled there and wrote his
History of Greece, and in 1852 built East Burnham Park, it is
said from the profits of his history, from which it was
known as 'History Hut'. It was there he and his wife were
visited by Mendelssohn, and by Alexis de Tocqueville.
During the 1939–45 War the Dutch Admiralty had their
headquarters there.

Farnham Royal is a pleasant little place whose most distinctive feature is the village pump, with its conical roof of
weathered red tiles, which, if the L.C.C. has its way, is
destined to increase enormously. William the Conqueror
granted the manor to Bertram de Verdon on the condition
of providing a glove for the king's right hand and supporting
his arm at the coronation, by which tenure of grand sergeanty the village became 'Royal'. The hereditary duty of
holding the King's right arm at the coronation was later
transferred to the Earls of Shrewsbury, and when Farnham
Royal was exchanged for Worksop the right to present a
glove was also transferred, although the traditional em-
broidery of the arms of Farnham Royal was retained. The
first Norman lord of Farnham Royal died at Joppa, on a
Crusade, and was buried at Acre.

The church was rebuilt in 1868, but retains a few monuments, including a brass to Eustace Mascoll, 'pistile reader' in
Windsor Castle, who died in 1567. He is said to have been
clerk of the works at the building of Christ Church, Oxford,
under the direction of Cardinal Wolsey. There is a mural to
Jacob Bryant, the antiquary, of Cippenham, but no monument commemorates Edward Chandler, author of the
Defence of Christianity, who was successively Bishop of
Lichfield, Lincoln and Durham, and died in London in 1750
'shamefully rich'.

A native of Farnham Royal, whose name was Dodd, is

Huntercombe Manor.

Kedermister Library, Langley Church

Stewkley Church

said to have been the original of Dickens' 'Golden Dustman', Boffin, in *Our Mutual Friend*.

The best approach from Slough to Stoke Poges is by Stoke Road, where the houses are quickly replaced by fields and cherry orchards. Fortunately, the National Trust are preserving the field beside the church with its monument to the poet, and the inspiration of a local magnate has transformed the land on the south into the beautifully planned Gardens of Remembrance, enchantingly lovely all through the year with a wealth of trees, flowers and rare flowering shrubs.

The neat churchyard, with its path lined with rose trees, is a charming setting for the grey flint walls of the church. The tower is no longer 'ivy-mantl'd', and the tall spire, which is so conspicuous in all old prints of the church, has been taken down and replaced by a small conical cap, but there are still old yew trees, and an air of settled peace. The tomb of Gray and his beloved mother is in the churchyard close by the East window. The church has been restored, but there is a Norman window, and other twelfth-century work. The timber south porch was built in the early fourteenth century, and the Hastings chapel about 1560.

There are wall monuments and tablets by Flaxman and Chantry; good brasses; old stained glass, some of it Flemish, and unusually good Victorian stained-glass windows, one of which is signed by Meyer of Munich.

All visitors to Stoke Poges church know of the *Elegy* it inspired, and some at least of the details of Gray's life; some of them also know that when Gray's friend, Lady Cobham, died the old manor-house was bought by the Hon. Thomas Penn, the second son of the founder of Pennsylvania, but knowledge of the history of its earlier owners is less widespread, although it has been associated with many famous people since the time of its first Saxon owner. It was the marriage of the thirteenth-century heiress, Amicia de Stokes, with Roger de Pogeis which gave the manor its name. In 1331, Sir John Molines, Marshal of the King's Falcons and Supervisor of the Queen's Castles, came into possession of the manor. He was an active, clever self-seeker who made a wealthy marriage, and played an important part in political affairs during the reign of Edward III. A series of heiresses carried the manor eventually to the Earl of Huntingdon, who built the old manor-house, the surviving west wing of which is close to the church. It was in this house that some of the Hatton family lived.

About 1600, Sir Edward Coke, afterwards Lord Chief Justice, leased the manor. He entertained Queen Elizabeth there the following year and lived in the house until his death in 1634. Sir Edward Coke, a great patriot, an outstanding lawyer and shining light even in the Elizabethan era, was easily the most famous man who lived at Stoke Park, but there is a shadow over his occupancy in the many quarrels with his wife and her beloved daughter Frances. Lady Elizabeth's first husband was Sir Christopher Hatton. A legend retold by Richard Barham in *The Housewarming*, one of the *Ingoldsby Legends*, recounts how she was carried away by the Devil from a party at Hatton House, in Holborn, leaving behind only her bleeding heart in the pump yard outside, from which fact Bleeding House Yard is said to derive its name. How the legend can be reconciled with her second marriage is not explained! The story of Lady Elizabeth and her daughter, as reconstructed from contemporary letters and documents, is fascinatingly told by Laura Norsworthy in *The Lady of Bleeding Heart Yard*.

It was in 1760 that Thomas Penn bought the estate. His son, John, pulled down all but one wing of the old manor-house, and built the enormous eighteenth-century mansion now known as Stoke Park, designed in 1789 by Wyatt and Nasmith, with grounds laid out by Repton and Brown, and later remodelled by Penn himself. Although John Penn was a bachelor, among many other activities he founded a 'matrimonial society' in 1817, with the object of improving the domestic life of married couples. He also erected a column to the memory of Coke, and the monument to Gray. His brother, Granville, who succeeded him, was the last Penn to own the estate. It was during his ownership that Sir Edwin Landseer worked there, and it is said a stag in Stoke Park furnished the original for his well-known picture *The Monarch of the Glen.*

West End House, where Gray lived from 1742 to 1753, is incorporated in Stoke Court, a mile away to the north, on the outskirts of Stoke Poges village. Among other mansions in the neighbourhood is Stoke Place, in grounds with an ornamental lake laid out by 'Capability' Brown in 1771.

Fulmer can be reached by the road which runs from Stoke Poges to Stoke Common, where there is a road running along the northern edge of the Common to Fulmer, but the ideal approach to this delightful village is by way of Wexham Street, which can be reached from Stoke Poges by a short road skirting Stoke Place, passing another of the picturesque country 'pubs' in which the neighbourhood is happily so rich.

The small flint church at Wexham has a nave dating from the twelfth century, and a modern but extremely picturesque wooden bell turret and spire. Small and remote though it is, Wexham has had some distinguished rectors. Edward Waddington, afterwards Bishop of Chichester, was rector from 1702 to 1706, and his successor, William Fleetwood, one of the most celebrated preachers of his day, and a generous patron of letters, was himself the author of many books and sermons. His best known and most valuable work, *Chronicon Pretiosum*, which gives accurate information on the value of money and price of commodities for the previous six centuries, was written at Wexham. He became Bishop of St. Asaph in 1708, and Bishop of Ely in 1714.

There is a sixteenth-century timber-framed outbuilding at the old manor-house, now Wexham Court Farm, which lies just across the road from the church, and parts of three Saxon homestead moats.

Modern houses have encroached on the outskirts of Wexham Woods, but there are still untouched areas of woodlands in the parish, some of which are famous locally for their bluebells.

The road to Fulmer, soon after passing the hamlet of Wexham Street with its duck-pond, gives a perfect view of Fulmer village in a hollow beside the tiny river Alderbourne, backed by a beautiful wooded ridge of the Chilterns. Although its few buildings are mostly of Victorian date, the model, yellow-washed cottages, the delightful inn, and the early seventeenth-century brick church, restored in the nineteenth century, are so well-grouped and attractive that it is wholly captivating.

In the church, which he built, there is a splendid monument to Sir Marmaduke Dayrell, with an inscription describing him as 'Servant to ye famous Queen Elizabeth in her warres both by sea and land and after in her Houshold' and also 'cofferer to King James of blessed memory, and dyed cofferer to ye excellent Prince King Charles, and favoured by all those renowned princes, and employed in matters of great trust for ye space of fifty yeares'.

The site of his great mansion is marked by the smaller Fulmer Place, built in the early eighteenth century by Richard Eskrigge, Sheriff of Buckingham, the great-grandfather of Sir Richard Owen, the eminent zoologist. The house was sold by Sir Richard's father some years before the zoologist was born, and the claim that he often visited Fulmer in his boyhood is apparently based on a visit he made fifty years after, when, as he tells us in his letters, he was welcomed kindly by the owner, and picked a leaf from an apple-tree for his sister.

CHAPTER SIX: *Along the Chess and the Coln*

IN its short eight miles the River Chess flows for the greater part of its journey through Buckinghamshire, reaching the Coln just over the Hertfordshire boundary near Rickmansworth. More than any of the other Chiltern rivers, it has suffered from exploitation, but its wealth of historical associations and delightful nooks and corners which have contrived to escape development make it well worth exploring.

The Chess wells up forcefully at Chesham among the water-cress beds in Bury Park.

Chesham church, nearby, is of Decorated and Perpendicular work, and has a curious monument to Richard Woodcote, a former vicar who died in 1623, with a Latin inscription describing him as 'a hammer of the heretics, in his life, a flash of lightning and his words full of stings'. It was in this church that the unfortunate Thomas Harding was compelled to stand before the congregation and hear the vicar preach against his alleged heresies on the day before he was burned to death in 1532 'in the dell going to Botley on the north end of the town of Chesham'. A later vicar was instrumental in having a cross erected in the churchyard in 1908, with an inscription to Harding's memory, and a quotation from Wycliff's Bible, the possession of which had been his chief crime.

A curious character associated with Chesham in the seventeenth century was Roger Crab, said to have been the original of the 'Mad Hatter' in Lewis Carroll's *Alice in Wonderland*. When he was about twenty, he began to restrict himself to a vegetarian diet, chiefly of roots and bran, dock-leaves and grass. He would not even eat butter and cheese,

57

and drank nothing but water. In his queer autobiography, *The English Hermite, or Wonder of this Age*, reprinted in the *Harleian Miscellanies*, he claimed to be able to live on three farthings a week. He opened a hat shop in Chesham, but shut it up in 1651, and settled in 'a small roode of ground', where he dabbled in astrology and physic and wrote his quaint tracts.

The older part of Chesham lies in a hollow of the hills, whose beechwoods provide the wood for the sawmills, and for the 'bodgers', who, among many other typical Buckinghamshire products, turn out wooden hoops and spades for children. The Chess, with its water-cress beds and ducks, provides other characteristic occupations, but newer industries have led to a great increase in population since the beginning of the twentieth century, and the newer town is not of the happiest design, whilst most of the charming old houses in the High Street have been incongruously modernized. High House dates from about the beginning of the seventeenth century, and numbers 54 and 56 Church Street, once a single house, date back in part to the fourteenth century. Lord's, one of the three cornmills on the Chess, dates from the seventeenth century.

'The Rolling Pin', near the churchyard, believed to be a prehistoric tumulus, and the ancient cultivation terraces known as 'the Balks', on the east of Chesham, point to the antiquity of the town.

Chesham is set at the junction of several valleys, and within a few miles to the north are Lee, whose church has one of the only five known bells by Michael de Wymbis—all of which are in Bucks—believed to date from 1290; Hawridge, with a rebuilt church beside the Manor Farm, in a prehistoric camp; Cholesbury, where the church is neighboured by a well-preserved plateau camp covering fifteen acres, and St. Leonards, which has a small but attractive old church.

South of Chesham is Chesham Bois, beautifully situated on a ridge dividing the Chess Valley from that of the Misbourne. It is a modern residential district now merged with the newer part of Amersham, and practically nothing but the restored church remains to remind the visitor that the village was in existence at least as early as the twelfth century. It was known as Boys in Cesteresham in 1276, and as Chesham Boys in the following century, and the old pronunciation is still retained.

The church dates chiefly from the fourteenth century. It has some old glass, and three good sixteenth-century brasses, one of which is to the infant son of Roger Lee, who died within a month of his baptism, and according to custom, was buried in the white cloth, or chrysom, in which infants were wrapped immediately after baptism, as recorded in the inscription to his memory.

Chesham Bois was the birthplace of Sir Arthur Lasenby Liberty, founder of the famous London store.

Farther down the valley the hills rise more steeply, with Latimer on the north and Chenies on the south. Latimer village, house, and church were almost entirely rebuilt in the Victorian era, but the drawing-room in Latimer House survives from the earlier house on the site, in which Charles I slept in 1647 as a prisoner, and his son Charles was entertained on the eve of his flight to the Continent. It was the birthplace of Hester Sandys, who became the wife of Sir Thomas Temple of Stowe, remembered only for Thomas Fuller's quaint reference in his *Worthies*: 'She had four sons and nine daughters which lived to be married, and so exceedingly multiplied, that this lady saw seven hundred extracted from her body. Reader I speak within compass, and have left myself a reserve, having bought the truth hereof by a wager I lost.'

The Chess forms an ornamental lake in the grounds of Latimer House, a large mansion of red brick built about the middle of the nineteenth century in the Tudor style. It is now a College. A bridge over the river gives access to the model village, set round a little green shaded by fine trees.

The brick church, designed by Sir Gilbert Scott, is set on a fir-clad hill, and has a few memorials from the older church on the site. The setting of Latimer is charming, and the immediate neighbourhood full of delightful walks.

Chenies, a mile and a half away across the river, is another model village with a well in the centre of the green, but here there is a fine inn. The Perpendicular church has a Norman font and good brasses. There is also an exceptionally interesting series of monuments in the Russell Chapel—but here again authority intervenes, and only by permission of the Woburn Estate can the chapel be entered, although its array of monuments, dating from 1484 onwards, can be glimpsed through the wrought-iron work separating it from the chancel. The monuments were minutely described by James Anthony Froude in his essay 'Chenies and the House of Russell', in *Short Studies on Great Affairs*. They are also described by Horace Walpole in a letter to George Montague in 1749:

'I have just seen a collection of tombs . . . the House of Russell robed in alabaster and painted. There are seven monuments in all; one is immense, in marble, cherubim'd and seraphim'd, crusted with bas-reliefs and titles for the first Duke of Bedford and his Duchess. All these are in a chapel of the church at Cheneys, the seat of the first earls.'

The great monument depicting the first Duke of Bedford and his Duchess shows them lamenting the untimely death of their son, Lord William Russell, who was sentenced to death for his alleged share in the Rye House Plot, a miscarriage of justice which was the direct cause of the overthrow of the Stuart dynasty and the welcoming of William of Orange to the English throne. The first Duchess had other sorrows, for when old and widowed she learned for the first time that her mother had planned the murder of Overbury in the Tower in order to marry Robert Carr, Earl of Somerset. Froude says, 'She was found senseless, with her hand upon the open page, and never rallied from the blow'.

Chenies was originally called Isenhampstead, after the twelfth-century lord of the manor, who was probably an ancestor of the Cheynes, who held the manor from the thirteenth century until the Russells acquired it by marriage in 1526. Leland, writing twelve years later, tells us:

'The olde house of the Cheyneis is so translated by my Lorde Russel, that hath this house in right of his wife, that litle or nothing remayneth untranslated: and a great deale of the house in ben newly set up, made of bricke and timber: and faire logginges be new erected in the gardein. The house is within divers Places richly painted with antique works of white and blak.'

The 'translated' house became the family home of the Russells until they removed to Woburn Abbey as their chief seat, and when Horace Walpole came over from Latimer in 1749 he found it in a state of dilapidation: 'There are but piteous fragments of the house remaining, now a farm, built round three sides of a court. It is dropping down in several places without a roof, but in half of the windows are beautiful arms in painted glass. As these are totally neglected, I propose making a push and begging them of the Duke of Bedford. They would be magnificent for Strawberry Castle.'

In spite of this dismal account, the wing which remains is in an excellent state of preservation, with quaintly twisted chimneys and high-gabled roofs reproduced in the cottages of the village, and as some of the original glass remains, it appears Horace Walpole did not succeed in securing any for his own house. An oak in the field in front of the manor-house is said to have been planted by Queen Elizabeth when she stayed there in 1570.

All the country round is hilly and densely wooded, and the Chess is famous for the trout-fishing in the neighbourhood.

Within a mile or two of Chenies, the River Chess, which has marked the boundary between Buckinghamshire and Hertfordshire since it left Latimer, flows across the county boundary to join the Coln near Rickmansworth.

ii

The River Coln rises in Hertfordshire, and flows for thirty-five miles to join the Thames at Wraysbury; for the greater part of which it forms the boundary between Buckinghamshire and Middlesex. It winds its way through alluvial flats very different from the valleys of the Chiltern rivers, and frequently divides into branches which reunite lower down. It is a quiet, pastoral landscape—never very exciting, but always charming.

The Coln makes it way through the grounds of Denham Court, and close by Uxbridge, where it splits into several branches, one of which flows close to the church at Iver, under a bridge shaded by fine trees and companioned by a Georgian house, which is an object lesson in the charm of perfect proportions. G. F. Bodley, the church architect, lived there from 1895 to 1905.

The church is of exceptional architectural interest, with a considerable amount of Saxon work surviving, and Roman brickwork in the eastern angle of the nave, and clear traces of work done in every following century up to the rebuilding in the latter half of the fifteenth century.

There are some brasses and monuments, the most imposing of which is one by Gerard Christmas, depicting Lady Mary Salter, who died in 1631, rising dramatically from her coffin. It has gained additional interest since the war, as other monuments to her family by Gerard Christmas, in Chelsea

Old Church, were destroyed in the bombing. One or two classical monuments are worth notice, and there are un- usually good eighteenth-century monuments in the church- yard. There is a tremendously long inscription to a hero killed in action in 1813, James Whitshed, an eighteen-year- old midshipman, which describes his death:

> 'His Time was short, and yet that honour'd name
> Shall live in memr'y and be dear to fame.
> NELSON, expiring, could have said no more
> Than he whose early Death these Lines deplore
> Leading his Band to Board his Country's foe
> Too true Alas! was aimed the Fatal Blow
> The Ball had pierced the youthful Hero's head,
> But ere to Heav'n his gallant spirit fled
> His look display'd a Soul despising death
> He cheer'd his Men and with convulsive breath
> Dying exclaimed amidst the Battle's roar
> Carry her if you can, my lads,
>   I am no more.'

Among numerous other monuments is a small effigy to John King, who was killed in 1603 by his kinsman Roger Parkinson, in a drunken brawl; a marble bust by Chantrey to Edward Ward, minister for thirty-one years. Elizabeth Kedermister, grand-daughter of Edmund Waller, the poet; and Admiral Lord Gambier, whose ship was the first to break the enemy's lines on 1 June 1794, are also commemor- ated in the church.

It was during Lord Gambier's retirement at Iver Lodge that experiments with wild heartsease carried out by Thompson, his head gardener—it is said at Lord Gambier's suggestion—formed the basis of the modern strains of pansies.

The village street running westward from the church still has a sixteenth-century inn and some seventeenth-century houses, but the rest of the parish consists chiefly of large houses, in their own grounds, which have been rebuilt in the nineteenth century, or entirely modern residential areas. The only remains of the old Elizabethan manor-house of the Pagets, which was pulled down in 1800, is a dove-house mentioned in 1743. A smaller house marks the site of the original mansion. The Pinewood Film Studios lie to the north, at Iver Heath.

Parsonage Farm, about a mile and a half to the south-west of the village, dates partly from the sixteenth century. An old homestead moat encloses house and garden, and there are two sixteenth-century barns.

Also on the south-west of Iver is the modern residential district developed on the estate of Richings Park, the eighteenth-century house in which the first Earl Bathurst entertained Addison, Pope, and other literary giants of his day. A description of Lord Bathurst in his old age, ready to please and to be pleased, is given in the third of Sterne's *Letters to Eliza*.

Later the house was bought by Lord Hertford, afterwards Duke of Somerset, who changed the name to Piercy Lodge, under which name it is frequently mentioned by Shenstone and other poets. Lady Hertford gave many details of the house and its surroundings in her later correspondence. She and her husband also entertained a number of poets, including Thomson, who dedicated his poem *Spring* to Lady Hertford, but gave great offence by carousing with Lord Hertford instead of assisting her ladyship to make poetry.

Edward Jesse, in his *Favourite Haunts and Rural Studies*, published in 1847, described a visit to Richings Park, and 'Parlem House', which had been minutely described by Lady Hertford. Now known as Parlaunt Park Farm, it is a sixteenth-century building surrounded by a lozenge-shaped homestead moat.

A road runs south from Richings Park to the junction of the Colnbrook by-pass and the old Bath Road, along which

Colnbrook is strung out. In the days of Henry VIII, Colnbrook was a municipal borough and market town, but lost
its charter in the seventeenth century, and the market has
long since ceased to exist. Nevertheless, it was a great
coaching station in the eighteenth and early nineteenth centuries, and still has some interesting old inns, the oldest of
which is the Ostrich Inn, probably built about 1500. There
is a good deal of seventeenth-century panelling inside, and in
a room on the first floor are the remains of a curious con-
trivance by which a flap could be let down from the window,
enabling travellers to enter the room from the top of a coach.

Lipscomb quotes a description of the murder of thirteen
people by the landlord of the Ostrich Inn, who disposed of
their bodies by throwing them into the River Coln nearby.
A pistol is still preserved which is said to have belonged to
Dick Turpin, who used this house. The George Inn, which
has the remains of sixteenth-century work, is said to have
derived its name from a wooden statue of St. George which
dropped off a wagon outside the inn. Princess Elizabeth
stayed there for a night in 1558 on her way from Woodstock
to Hampton Court as a prisoner. The seventeenth-century
Star and Garter also survives, but other historic inns have
disappeared, including the Catherine Wheel, mentioned in
one of Cromwell's letters, where Henry VIII and Queen
Catherine stayed in 1516, and Prince Rupert spent a night
over a century later. The White Hart Inn was associated
with the *Ballad of the Three Cooks of Colnbrook*, and the
earliest mention of Colnbrook, in 1106, refers to an inn kept
there by Ægelward, which was given to Abingdon Abbey in
recognition of the Abbot's skill as a physician.

Colnbrook constantly figured in history. Froissart's
Chronicles record that four ambassadors from Philip, King of
France, were sent to Edward III at Windsor in 1337 to do
homage for the Duchy of Guienne, and 'dyned in the
Kynge's chamber, and after they departed, and lay the same

night at Colebrook'. The conspirators against Henry IV in 1400 met at Colnbrook, and it was mentioned in connexion with Queen Jane's funeral in 1537. The petition of the Lords and Commons for peace after the Battle of Edgehill in 1642 were presented to the King at Colnbrook, and soon afterwards Prince Rupert plundered the town.

Pepys dined there in June of 1668; and Defoe recounts at length the alarms and excursions at 'Colebrook' and the wild rumours which accompanied the approach of the Prince of Orange and his army, and the flight of James II.

Part of Colnbrook is in the county of Middlesex, across the Coln, near which is the half-timbered building traditionally known as King John's Palace. The old parish church disappeared long since, and its site is not even marked by the Victorian church. Tan House Farm is the Old Manor-House, where the Lord of the Manor held his Court, and has an interesting Elizabethan tithe barn constructed of teak taken from a Spanish galleon. The barn is the largest of that date surviving in Bucks. In the coaching days, when highwaymen were at the height of their activities, a number of them were executed in the market-place and buried on the spot. Human remains were found during excavations carried out in 1935.

In the more peaceful days of the early nineteenth century Cox's Orange Pippin was raised at Colnbrook Lawn by a retired brewer, and first put on the market in 1825.

The village of Horton is not much more than a mile southwest of Colnbrook, in meadows near the Coln. It is still strangely peaceful and secluded, in spite of its proximity to the Great West Road and the riverside resort of Wraysbury. Its only claim to fame—but that a supreme one—is that it was the home of Milton for six years, during which he wrote his earlier poems, and enshrined his impressions of the countryside in *Il Penseroso*, *Song on May Morning*, *Comus*, *Lycidas*, and *L'Allegro*, in the latter of which he writes of:

'Meadows trim, with daisies pied;
Shallow brooks, and rivers wide;
Towers and battlements it sees
Bosomed high in tufted trees . . .'

which is still a perfect description of Horton and its view of Windsor Castle.

Berkin Manor, which was built in the nineteenth century, is believed to mark the site of the house rented by Milton's father in 1632, of which only a red-brick dovecote survives. Milton's mother died there in 1637, and was buried in the parish church. His father and brother Christopher remained in Horton until 1640, and there is a record of the death of Christopher's infant son, and the baptism of his daughter Sarah. David Masson reconstructs all the quiet events of Milton's life at Horton in his *Life of Milton*, in which he brought to light every possible incident of those six years.

The Elizabethan mansion known as Place House was taken down in 1785, but some very picturesque farms survive in the neighbourhood. The Early English church has a richly ornamented Norman north door and a fine Decorated wooden porch. Sarah Milton's grave is marked by a flat stone in the chancel floor, and the East window has Victorian stained glass by Kempe, dedicated to Milton, with a panel in one of the lancets depicting him writing *Paradise Lost*.

THE Chiltern Hills run south-westward from the borders of Suffolk to Oxfordshire, but the greater part is in Buckinghamshire, and the whole of the three Chiltern Hundreds are in that county. Over a thousand years ago the twelfth abbot of St. Albans granted lands to Thurnoth, on condition that he protected the district from bandits and gave safe escort to the monks and pilgrims to the abbey, but in spite of the efforts of the Saxon knight and his successors, they remained such a haunt of bandits, that the saying grew up in Buckinghamshire 'If you beat a bush, a robber will appear'. Such names as Gallows Hill, Hang Alley, and Hangings Lane perpetuate the rough justice meted out to the robbers, but still they persisted, and for centuries the Steward of the Chiltern Hundreds received considerable sums in fines, in addition to the rents, fees, and tolls paid at the Hundred Courts.

Later, as conditions changed, the Hundred courts lost their importance, and by 1679 the Stewardship of the Chiltern Hundreds was farmed out for thirty-one years at a yearly rent of £1 6s. 8d., and a fine of £150—the annual income being £18 6s. 8d., and from this arose the modern association with Parliament, when a member wishing to vacate his seat applies for the office of Steward of the Chiltern Hundreds. The House of Commons passed a resolution in 1623 'that a man, after he is duly chosen, cannot relinquish his membership'. This rule, necessary when country gentlemen had frequently to be compelled to represent their shire in Parliament, continues in force, but as a member of the House of Commons who accepts 'any office of profit from the Crown' ceases to be a member, the custom grew up of applying for the Stewardship, in a truly English compromise.

The Chiltern Hills are composed chiefly of chalk, and William Camden, the great antiquary, thought their name was akin to the British word 'cylt' or 'chilt', meaning chalk. The Britons have left many traces of the centuries when they lived in these hills, where they maintained their independence long after the Saxons were settled in the Thames valley. The Icknield Way, which follows the northern edge, is probably of British origin, and more than one writer has noted the large proportion of people in the Chilterns who are small-bodied, with small, dark faces and dark hair and eyes—a distinctive type believed to be due to a strong strain of British blood left from those far-off days.

The northern face of the Chilterns rises in an abrupt escarpment above the Vale of Aylesbury, but the southern hills descend very gradually, in exquisite, rounded contours, to the Thames valley. The predominating trees are beech, for which the county is so famous, but there are also mixed woods of oak, hazel, and fir, and the delicate charm of silver birch. It is a country to inspire men with thoughts of freedom, and with exquisite poetry. Here every movement against oppression has found supporters. It was a stronghold of the Lollards and of the Quakers; it saw Hampden's struggle for the liberty of the subject; and many another noble cause has been fostered in these hills.

Here, too, the 'bodger', or wood-worker, still lingers on, working in the woods, and old dialects survive in such words as 'pimmocky', meaning fastidious; 'kurlick' for charlock, and other Bucks expressions, many of which are recorded in Mr. H. Harman's book on *Bucks Dialect*.

The one great drawback has been the fatal proximity of the Chilterns to London, which has had an irresistible temptation for haphazard development, particularly during the period between the wars. Badly designed rows of houses are unfortunate enough at Slough, on level ground beside the Bath road, but they become an outrage when they spoil the skyline of such lovely, rounded hills as the Chilterns.

Fortunately, in almost every case modern developments have left the older town untouched, and the greater part of the Chiltern Hills are still so isolated that the small villages in their narrow and supremely beautiful valleys are like a survival from an earlier age, as remote as the most fanatical lover of solitude could wish.

ii

The River Misbourne rises near Great Missenden, and flows fourteen miles south-east to the Coln, near Uxbridge. Its actual source is difficult to discover, and history records that it has changed its course more than once—each change being said to presage a national disaster. Sometimes part of the river disappears altogether for several years. Its name— a blending of the British 'maes', a field, and the Saxon 'bourne', a river—is singularly appropriate for a river whose course is frequently marked solely by a grass-grown dip in the fields. Nevertheless, the valley, with or without its river, has a very great charm in those areas where it has not been developed.

The upper valley has been fortunate enough to retain its old-time peace and beauty, and Great Missenden is still much as Leland described it in the reign of Henry VIII: 'a preaty thoroughfare, but no market-toun', though a great abbey, founded by William de Missenden in 1133, survives only in a few traces of thirteenth-century work incorporated in the modern abbey on the site.

Great Missenden Abbey of Black Canons was one of the largest and most important in Bucks. It saw more than one event not commonly associated with life in a monastery. Hugh de Plessetis, lord of the manor in the thirteenth century, was buried in the church, at his own wish, together with his white palfrey 'Principal', his armour, and the horse's harness. In 1297 a novice cut his throat 'for fear of discipline'; the abbot was deprived of his office after a visit by Bishop Grosseteste in 1236; and another of the abbots was hanged for clipping the coinage of Edward III!

It is pleasant to know that Henry Honor lived up to his name when he was abbot, and compiled a *chartulary* of the abbey which is a valuable source of information, giving details of the grants, properties and privileges of the monks, and 'medical' prescriptions, which included 'oil of black snails', 'marrow of horse bones' and other nauseous concoctions.

In 1530 there was another scandal when Abbot John Fox faced heavy charges against his community, one of whom 'had been seen more than once at midnight coming out of a house in the village in doublet and jerkin, with a sword by his side'. The last abbot, John Ottwell, accepted the inevitable and returned to everyday life at the Dissolution, with a pension of £50 a year, and one of the monks, Thomas Barnard, was inducted to the vicarage of Great Missenden.

The newer part of Great Missenden climbs the hillside above the older part of the town bordering the London to Aylesbury road, and is now linked up with Prestwood, and the church is also high on a beech-covered hill above the town. Its superb situation, looking down on the park of Missenden Abbey, and its fine proportions internally, make the climb up the steep hillside well worth while. Though much restored, it has a Norman font, mural monuments and brasses, and old encaustic tiles found in the abbey grounds. One of the brasses dates from 1450, and another depicts the bust of a woman with plaited hair which does not seem to have any connexion with the inscription below. One of the murals is the only example in the county of work by the seventeenth-century sculptor, Nicholas Stone.

James Stephen, the friend of Wilberforce, whose sister he married as his second wife, built himself a house on Frith

Hill at Great Missenden about 1816, where he lived until his death seventeen years later, and was frequently visited there by his brother-in-law. He left six children by his first wife. William was vicar of Bledlow for nearly sixty years; Henry John was a serjeant-at-law and a distinguished and able writer on legal subjects; Sir James became a colonial Under-secretary, and for many years 'literally ruled the colonial empire', his influence gaining for him the nickname of 'King Stephen'; and Sir George wrote and worked exten-sively in the cause of anti-slavery, and also wrote two novels popular in their day, *Adventures of a Gentleman in Search of a Horse*, and *Adventures of an Attorney in Search of a Practice*. Two grandsons of James Stephen also achieved distinction. Sir James Fitzjames Stephen, the Judge, and Sir Leslie Stephen, and two great-grandsons, Sir Herbert and James Kenneth Stephen, achieved high honours in their chosen spheres—a notable record for one family.

William Black, another popular novelist of the Victorian era, frequently visited Great Missenden, having married the sister of one of the Honor family there.

Glorious beechwoods still extend nearly all the three miles between Great Missenden and Great Hampden, which passes the large stone cross, on a field of Honor End Farm, which was set up in 1863 to commemorate the refusal of John Hampden to pay ship money on these lands. The handful of cottages and the inn which make up the hamlet of Great Hampden are on the border of the wild common of Hamp-den, backed and bordered with dense beechwoods, with the house and church nearly a mile away, approached through an avenue of beech and sweet chestnut.

The Hampden family were granted the estates at the Con-quest, and they have descended since John Hampden's day, in the female line to the Earls of Buckinghamshire. The house is a large, battlemented eighteenth-century building incorporating some of the fourteenth-century mansion on the site, and a considerable amount of Jacobean work. It is now a girls' school.

The most famous of all the noble family of Hampden is, of course, John Hampden, believed to have been born in London in 1594, but whose associations with Buckingham-shire were extremely close throughout his life. His first wife, Elizabeth Simeon, lies in the church, with an inscription he wrote himself:

'In her pilgrimage
The staie and comfort of her neighbours,
The love and glory of a well-ordered family,
The delight and happiness of tender parents,
But a crowne of blessings to a husband
In a wife: to all an eternal pattern of
Goodness and cause of Joy; whilst She was
In her dissolution

A loss unvaluable to each, yet herself blest, and they fully recompenc'd in her translation from a tabernacle of claye and fellowship with mortalls to a Celestial Mansion and Communion with a Deity, the 20th day of August,
1634.

John Hampden, her sorrowful Husband, in perpetual memory of his conjugall love, hath erected this Monument.'

It was a year later that his refusal to pay ship-money in Great Kimble church made him the cynosure of all eyes, and won for him the title of 'Patriot' which not even his enemies denied him. The cousin of Oliver Cromwell and Edmund Waller, it was natural he should fight on the side of the Parliamentarians, and he did good service, until he received the fatal wound on Chalgrove Field in 1643.

The hall of Great Hampden House, known as the 'brick parlour', is traditionally the one where Hampden received the Commissioners sent to arrest him, and in it are preserved his helmet and communion cup and other relics, and a magnificent collection of portraits, including one of John Hampden. The memorial to his memory in Great Hampden church, with a relief showing him receiving his death-wound on Chalgrove Field, was put up a century after his death. Although an account of his funeral, and burial with full military honours in the parish church, appeared in a contemporary newspaper, *The Kingdome's Weekly Intelligencer*, the exact spot in which he is buried is unknown, in spite of researches made by his biographer, Lord Nugent, in 1928. Queen's Gap, on the Hampden estate, recalls the visit of Queen Elizabeth, having been made to facilitate her approach from Oxford. The ground was levelled by throwing the bank of Grim's Dyke into the ditch.

A mile away, on the Great Missenden road, is the site of a tree known for centuries as the King's Beech, under which Edward III and the Black Prince are said to have administered justice when on their way to visit the Hampden of that day. An apocryphal story that the Black Prince and one of his host's sons quarrelled over a game of tennis gave rise to a rhyme:

> 'Tring, Wing, and Ivinghoe
> Hampden of Hampden did foregoe
> For striking of ye prynce a blow,
> And glad he might escape it so.'

As the Hampden family never owned these manors, they could not have forfeited them, so it is difficult to see how the idea ever arose.

Hampden is described under the name of Burnham in William Black's novel *Kilmeny*. John Masefield, the Poet Laureate, once made his home nearby at Hampden Row, where he wrote his famous poem *The Everlasting Mercy*.

Little Hampden lies almost buried in beechwoods, seemingly right out of the world. The simple but pleasant little church has an interesting two-storied south porch and important mural paintings discovered in 1907, some of which are believed to date from the reign of Henry III.

Returning to the valley of the Misbourne after this wandering down Chiltern by-ways to the past, we make our way along the two and a half miles which lead to Little Missenden, where the River Misbourne begins to take itself a little more seriously. Happy in being by-passed by the main road, it is a delightful little village grouped round its church and manor-house. The church, so unpretentious on the outside, has remarkable treasures in its bells and wall-paintings. The earliest of the fine peal of five bells is dated 1350, and the unusually fine and complete wall-paintings, uncovered in 1931, range from the late twelfth to the early fourteenth century. The manor-house, neighbouring the churchyard, was the home for many years of Dr. Bates, one of the members of the 'Knights of St. Francis' who met at Medmenham abbey, who repeatedly refuted the scandalous stories circulated about them. Lipscomb says, 'This testimony is the more valuable, as delivered by a gentleman of unimpeachable honour and veracity, at the distance of so many years after the consequence of opposite sentiments could have in any degree affected his reputation.'

There is a charming field path to Amersham, which runs through the park of Shardeloes, along the side of the ornamental lake and in full view of the ancient home of the Drake family. The plain but well-proportioned mansion, built by Stiff Leadbetter in 1758, has interior decorations by Robert Adam, and has remained almost untouched. It marks the site of the earlier mansion in which Queen Elizabeth was entertained by William Tothill. His daughter and heiress, Joan, the eldest of thirty-three children, married Francis Drake of Esher, about 1605, and founded the Buckinghamshire branch of the Drake family which has owned Shardeloes ever since.

Half a mile from Shardeloes is Amersham, the older part of which is the most perfect surviving example of the Buckinghamshire style of market town. The wide main street is flanked with seventeenth-century houses of a warm red brick varied by a few earlier buildings in colour-wash and timbering, and later work which harmonizes with the old-world atmosphere. The church is not outstanding architecturally, but houses a wealth of monuments, and the most beautiful seventeenth-century stained glass in the county.

Among the monuments are the work of several well-known eighteenth- and early nineteenth-century sculptors. The infant children of Chief Baron William Drake are commemorated by a graceful marble tablet, and another member of the Drake family who died young is commemorated by a quaint little brass dated 1623, showing a chubby four-year-old boy, with the inscription:

'Had hee liv'd to be a man
This inch had grown but to a span,
Now is hee past all feare of paine
'Twere sinn to wish him here againe.
Vewe but the way by wch wee come
Thow'l say hee's best that's first at home.'

William Grey, afterwards Bishop of Ely and High Treasurer of England, was rector of Amersham about 1437, and Edmund Waller, the poet, was baptised in the church. He was M.P. for Amersham at the age of sixteen! Another famous man who represented the Borough in Parliament was Algernon Sidney, brother of the famous Dorothy Sidney, Waller's 'Saccharissa'.

Among famous natives of Amersham were Walter de Agmondesham (the old name for Amersham), who was Chancellor of England in the reign of Edward I, and joined with the Bishop of Caithness in settling the rights of the claimants for the crown of Scotland after the death of the

Maid of Norway; and John of Amersham, a monk of St. Albans, described by Fuller in his *Worthies* as 'pious, painful, and a profound scholar'.

Arthur Machen, whose exquisite prose has charmed so many, lived at Amersham during the last years of his life, and is buried with his wife in the cemetery.

Amersham was a great centre for Lollards and Puritans, and there is a tradition that John Knox once occupied the pulpit in the church. Another great divine associated with the church was Richard Baxter, who held a public disputation with the Anabaptist soldiers of the Parliamentarian army. Among those burned at Amersham as heretics was William Tylsworth, the Lollard, whose own daughter was cruelly compelled to light the faggots.

J. K. Fowler, in his *Echoes of Old Country Life*, describes a curious local custom: 'The inns in the town were taken possession of at election time by the women-folk, old and young, married and unmarried—the two best inns being selected by the lady inhabitants. Here the fair ones awaited the arrival of the newly elected members who formally entered the room and very deliberately and demurely kissed them in turns. This performance concluded, a raid was made into the inn-rooms by the young men of the place, and amid loud laughter and screams and struggles innumerable, they also kissed the not unwilling dames'—a custom worthy of the Muggletonian Elections, which died out when the borough was disfranchised in 1832.

Bury Farm, at the east end of the town, was the home of Mary Penington in 1666, when her husband was imprisoned for his Quaker opinions.

Chalfont St. Giles is only three miles from Amersham, the pleasant road passing the Vache park, where the family of De la Vache lived in the fourteenth century. The property was sold to Thomas Fleetwood in 1564, but reverted to the Crown on the attainder of Colonel George Fleetwood, one of the signatories to the warrant for the execution of Charles I. His cousin, George Fleetwood, was also a distinguished Parliamentarian officer, who was tried as a regicide in 1661 and, like his cousin, escaped the death sentence with difficulty, but his uncle William was a Royalist, and not only acted as Chaplain to the King's army, but was also appointed guardian of the young princes at the battle of Edgehill. He was made Chaplain to Charles II at the Restoration, and later appointed Bishop of Worcester.

The Vache, said to have been built originally in the year 1277, has been almost entirely rebuilt in modern times. In the park is an eighteenth-century monument erected by the then owner, Sir Hugh Palliser, to his friend Captain Cook, with the inscription 'To the Memory of Captain James Cook, the ablest and most renowned navigator this or any other country has produced'.

The cottage where Milton found refuge from the plague, and completed *Paradise Lost*, has been carefully restored by the Milton Trustees, who have turned it into a museum of Milton relics, which include rare and valuable editions of his works. It is believed that there has been but little alteration since Milton lived there, and very fortunately the immediate surroundings have also changed comparatively little.

The church, of Norman foundation, has retained some Norman work, although remodelled in later centuries, and has interesting features, but its supreme attraction is the splendid series of fourteenth- and fifteenth-century wall paintings, which are the finest in the county, and deal with a number of subjects. Buried in the churchyard is Bertram Mills, founder of the famous circus.

Chalfont St. Peter lies two miles farther down the Misbourne Valley, the road passing under the woods of Newland Park. Abraham Newland, who built the house, was the chief cashier of the Bank of England, and the five-pound

notes of the day, bearing his signature, were known as New-
lands, which was commemorated in a popular song written
by the younger Charles Dibdin.

Chalfont St. Peter, less fortunate than its sister village, has
been almost lost in modernization and development, which
has included the demolition of interesting old houses, one at
least of which had extremely fine wall-paintings. Nevertheless, the large green is still bounded by pleasant houses. The
Greyhound Inn is a picturesque old building curiously set
over the River Misbourne, with part of its foundations on
an island in mid-stream. The church has interesting brasses,
including the palimpsest brass of a priest.

The Grange is a modern house marking the site of the
home of Isaac Penington and his family from 1657 to 1665,
during which time it was ever open to all members of the
Society of Friends. The Peningtons were an ideal Quaker
family, mild, kind, cultured, and deeply religious, with the
most tender love for each other and for their friends. Thomas
Ellwood, the young tutor of their children and trusted
guardian of Gulielma Springett, daughter of Mary Penington by her first husband, on journeys to visit relatives and
friends, has told the story of his conversion to Quakerism
and his happy life in that household, and of his work as
secretary to Milton, with unconscious charm in his *Autobiography*. A later work, *The Penns and Peningtons of the
Seventeenth Century* by Maria Webb, based on original
family letters, and other memoirs, has made their delightful circle alive for us to-day. Not the least charming is the
story of the courtship of William Penn, the founder of
Pennsylvania, and Guli Springett, whose ideal marriage was
the reflection of their truly admirable characters. *The Dictionary of National Biography* says of Penn: 'As a stout champion of the right of independent thought and speech, as the
apostle of true religion, of justice, gentleness, sobriety, sim-
plicity, and "sweet reasonableness" in an age of corrupt

splendour, morose pietism, and general intolerance, Penn would be secure of a place among the immortals, even though no flourishing state of the American Union revered him as its founder,' and Guli has always been acclaimed as a woman who was 'as good as she was beautiful'.

All who have felt the enduring attraction of Penns and Peningtons must rejoice that they are united in their last resting-place in the graveyard of the little Meeting-House at Jordans where they worshipped—still simple and unadorned as they loved it, and still apart in a tranquil setting of the quiet hills and glorious woods they knew.

The Misbourne flows south of Chalfont St. Peter through the grounds of Chalfont Park, which was rebuilt by Colonel Charles Churchill, brother-in-law of Horace Walpole, who often stayed at 'my sister's, at Chaffont'. Among the many fine trees in the park is an ash-tree 25 feet in circumference, and the old walled garden has been transformed by Sir Edwin Lutyens into an extremely beautiful Italian garden.

There is a path through the park to Denham, four and a half miles from Chalfont St. Peter, which has had the good fortune to retain its original beautiful village almost intact, although there is a formidable amount of unplanned development on its outskirts, and the great Denham film studios lie north of the railway, on the county boundary.

It is truly remarkable that a village within half an hour of London by train should remain so perfect, and, as so often in these cases, it is due to the influence of the great landowners of the neighbourhood. Whatever else can be said about the old type of landowners, they were at least almost invariably on the side of the angels in preserving the beauty of England.

The mellow brick houses, half-hidden in wistaria and climbing roses, line the winding road crossed by the Misbourne, now quite a respectable little river as it flows to join the Coln below Denham Court.

Denham Place, built about 1688 by Sir Roger Hill, and

altered in 1830, is on the site of the earlier home of the Peck-
hams, to whom there are monuments and brasses in the
parish church. A chapel in the north wing has beautifully
carved early sixteenth-century woodwork said to have been
brought from Somerset. There is a local tradition that Sir
Roger Hill hid the body of a footman he had murdered in a
secret room of Denham Place, but no trace of such a room
remains. Sir Roger's grandson, Benjamin Way, was a friend
of Captain Cook.

A fine avenue of limes shades the drive through the
grounds of Denham Court to the stately mansion with its
seventeenth-century west wing, all that remains of the older
mansion rebuilt in the two following centuries. The Coln,
which marks the boundary between Buckinghamshire and
Middlesex, flows through the beautiful grounds, and the
ancient fishponds still exist. Denham Court was for centuries the home of the Bowyers, who were granted the
manor of Denham in 1596. There is a tradition that Margaret Weld, wife of Sir William Bowyer, the first baronet,
hid Charles II in the house, and a series of pictures commemorates the event, but a comparison of dates and proba-
bilities seems to disprove the claim. The house has given
hospitality to Dryden, Dr. Johnson, Sir Humphry Davy,
George IV, and other celebrities. Dryden's wife was a kins-
woman of Lady Bowyer, and he wrote parts of some of his
most famous works when staying in the house, and also
composed his *Ode on St. Cecilia's Feast* in the grounds. He
declared, 'Nature had conspired with art to make the garden
one of the most delicious spots in England'.

Among other charming houses in the village are the
seventeenth-century Hill House, and a private house bearing
an inscription recording that it was founded as a school by
Sir William Bowyer in 1721, but the most interesting house
in the district is the Savoy, a mile north of the village on the
banks of the Coln, a moated house incorporating the remains

of an aisled hall dating from the fourteenth century. It was the home of Lady Cynthia Mosley, who is buried in the grounds, in a white marble tomb designed by Sir Edwin Lutyens.

Denham church has a fascinating array of monuments and brasses to the great families associated with Denham through the centuries, including one of the only two known brasses in England to an abbess, in memory of Dame Agnes Jordan, last abbess of Sion, and a palimpsest brass to a friar. There is also a rare example of an incised stone slab dated 1656 to Philip Edelen, and a fifteenth-century wall-painting of the Last Judgment.

CHAPTER EIGHT: *Around Beaconsfield*

THE older part of Beaconsfield is a perfect example of an eighteenth-century Buckinghamshire town, with its enormously wide streets, its picturesque brick-and-timber houses, and its splendid trees. Even the names of the streets have a pleasantly old-world sound, for they retain the ancient Buckinghamshire name of 'End': London End, Wycombe End, Aylesbury End, and Windsor End.

Incidentally, Beaconsfield's own name has long been a source of heated controversy, one school of thought claiming that it is derived from the Anglo-Saxon becken, a beech, and 'veldt', a clearing, meaning a clearing in the beechwoods, whilst others believe it to be derived from the Old English 'beacnes-feld', denoting open land marked by a beacon.

The Old Town abounds in houses dating from the early seventeenth century, although some have been re-faced. The White Hart Hotel, which was built about 1600, is an old coaching inn in whose visitors' book are the signatures of a host of celebrities. In one room is preserved a bust of G. K. Chesterton, who loved to sit there quaffing his ale and chatting with the company. The George Inn, also dating from about 1600, has been re-fronted, but has its original oak staircase, and a fireplace with chimney corners; the Old Swan Inn is a late sixteenth-century building, and the Saracen's Head, where the parlour used to be used as a police court, is, like the neighbouring Greyhound, of seventeenth-century work.

The most interesting building in Beaconsfield, however, is the Old Rectory, overlooking the churchyard. It is an exceptionally fine and untouched specimen of an early sixteenth-century timbered building. Inside are a wainscoted room and an oak staircase, with the arms of Burnham Abbey, which held Beaconsfield Manor for many centuries, in one of the chimney-pieces. The house contains some interesting old furniture, an original painting by Andrea del Sarto of *The Espousal of the Virgin*, and a fine copy of *The Martyrdom of St. Peter Martyr*, by Titian, the original of which was burned in 1867.

The church was probably built in the latter part of the fifteenth century, but has been so rebuilt and restored that it is practically a Victorian building. There are two seventeenth-century oak chairs, and an unusually fine example of a seventeenth-century iron chest with small painted landscapes between the bands, and interesting tombs and brasses.

The two most famous men associated with Beaconsfield are buried there: Edmund Burke, and his wife and much-loved son, are remembered by a simple marble tablet in the church, and Edmund Waller has a conspicuous tomb in the churchyard, with lengthy and fulsome eulogies.

Waller was born at Coleshill Manor-House, a few miles to the north, in 1606, but Wallers had been settled at Beaconsfield as early as the fourteenth century, and it was this perhaps which caused Edmund Waller and his widowed mother to buy Hall Barn in 1624. All trace of the house Edmund Waller knew is lost, but the lovely park and gardens owe much of their beauty to him.

In remembering Edmund Waller's changeable politics, it must be remembered also that he was a poet, with all the sensitiveness of a poet, and lived in extremely difficult times, which makes it hard to estimate him fairly. It would appear that he and his family were royalists at heart, but his relationship with Oliver Cromwell, though so distant, and his admiration for Cromwell's intellect, must have also had their influence.

During Edmund Waller's exile for his share in 'Waller's Plot' his mother managed his affairs at Hall Barn, and appar-

Burnham Beeches

Stoke Poges Church

Chalfont St. Giles Church

ently was much exercised in her mind over a husband for one
of her grand-daughters, writing to tell him about one of the
suitors: 'The young man is about 22 years old, yet he has
buryed a wife . . . I can have him for £2000 . . . but I am not
in a hurry to marry hir, she is younge enough to stay but the
danger is if she should catch the small poxe or hir beauty
should change. . . .'

Waller had a ready wit, which made him a favourite at
the courts of Charles II and James II and on occasion served
to extract him from a delicate situation. When Charles II
pointed out that the congratulatory address on his restoration to the throne was inferior, as a poem, to that which
Waller had addressed to Cromwell, he retorted: 'Poets,
Sire, succeed better in fiction than in truth'. Much of his
poetry was more easily appreciated in his own day for its
appositeness, but he will always be remembered for his exquisite *Go Lovely Rose*, and for some of the charming verses
he addressed to Lady Dorothy Sidney under the name of
Saccharissa.

Waller spent the last ten years of his life in retirement at
Hall Barn, where he died. His descendants held the property
until 1844, when it was sold to Sir Gore Ouseley, who
brought from Italy the wonderful seventeenth-century oak
carving of the Lodge opening on to Windsor End.

Burke's connection with Beaconsfield began when he
bought the estate of Gregories in 1768. He loved to retire
there from the excitements of his political career and live the
life of a country squire, pictured by Lord Morley in his
Biography: '. . . he would with his own hands give food to a
starving beggar, or medicine to a peasant sick of the ague;
where he would talk of the weather, the turnips, and the hay,
with the wain-men and the farm-bailiff; and where in the evening stillness he would pace the walk under the trees and reflect
on the state of Europe and the distractions of his country'.
With true Irish hospitality, he entertained his illustrious

friends there—Gratton, Hutchison, Fox and Sheridan, Mirabeau, Barry, Garrick, Sir Joshua Reynolds and Dr. Johnson, whilst Crabbe the poet was rescued from a debtor's prison, given generous aid, and encouraged to continue his career as a poet.

His generosity to the less fortunate was proverbial, although so often embarrassed for ready money himself, but not all his visitors approved of his happy-go-lucky Irish household, for Mrs. Piozzi wrote rather disparagingly of their family life 'among dirt, cobwebs, pictures, and statues', and of a negro servant who 'carried tea about with a cut finger wrapped in rags'.

It was on a visit to Gregories that Sir Joshua Reynolds saw the infant son of Burke's farm bailiff, and took him as a model for his picture *The Infant Hercules*.

After the death of his brother and son in the same year, 1794, Burke's career was broken and his happiness vanished for ever. 'I am torn up by the roots and lie frustrated in the earth,' he said. Three years later, he was dead himself.

It is said that it was out of reverence for Burke's memory that Disraeli, who had no personal link with Beaconsfield, took its name for his title.

Gregories, which Burke had renamed Butler's Court, was burned down in 1813, and the site is now largely built over, although Gregories Farmhouse still remains.

On the outskirts of Beaconsfield, towards London, are the gates of Wilton Park, an early Georgian building said to have been restored by Adam. There is a tumulus in the park, known as the Mount.

Modern Beaconsfield can also boast association with a celebrity, for it was the home of G. K. Chesterton for the last years of his life. Near the station is the Bekonscot Model Village and Railway, laid out in an attractive rock garden, which attracts thousands of visitors every year. It is modelled on a scale of about an inch to a foot, and covers about

1,250 square yards, with 1,200 ft. of railway track controlled by electricity.

ii

There is much of beauty and interest in the neighbour-hood of Beaconsfield, and it is possible to find by-ways through unspoiled country to Hedsor, Cliveden and Cook-ham, to Burnham village, or Hedgerley and Stoke Poges on the south, or to Jordans and beyond on the east, but on the north modern Beaconsfield extends nearly to Penn.

Penn itself is still an object-lesson in the charm of suitable materials well designed and perfectly placed. Set on high ground, three miles from the centre of old Beaconsfield, it has splendid views over the Thames Valley to the Berkshire Downs.

There have been Penns seated at Penn since 1222, many of whom are buried in the church, and attempts have been made to decide whether they were ancestors of the founder of Pennsylvania. His father, Admiral Sir William Penn, was a younger son of a family which had been settled for many generations at Minety in Gloucestershire, but on his tomb in St. Mary Redclyffe, Bristol, is an inscription claiming he was the son of 'Giles Penn, of the Penns of Penn Lodge, in the county of Wilts, and those Penns of Penn in the county of Bucks.' Six grandchildren of the founder of Pennsylvania are buried in Penn church.

The earliest part of the church dates from the fourteenth century, and the whole building has a charm which matches the village. There is a fine fifteenth-century wooden roof in the nave, and a contemporary painting of the Doom, on wood, found in 1938, hangs in the south aisle. The plain leaden font is a rare example of a font in this metal. There are curious rhymes on boards, a remarkably fine series of brasses to the Penns, ranging from 1540 to 1638, and a number of monuments and murals, some of which commemorate the Curzons, to whom the property passed by marriage in 1731.

On a clear day the church tower commands an extensive view, said to include twelve counties.

Penn is practically joined up with the village of Tyler's Green on the north, near the pond of which stood Tyler's Green House, pulled down about 1822. It was once the home of General William Haviland, who served under Wolfe at Quebec. In this house Edmund Burke founded a school in 1796 for the children of those Royalists who had died in the French Revolution. It continued in existence until 1820, and the site is still known as French School Meadow.

The village of Penn Street lies in beautiful woods of beech, oak, and ash, about two miles north of Penn. It has a modern church and rectory. In the grounds of Penn House is the mast of the ship commanded by Admiral Lord Howe, one of Nelson's Admirals, on which his flag is flown every year on 'the glorious first of June', the anniversary of the battle of 1794. It was his daughter who married Penn Assheton Curzon and brought the title to the Curzons of Penn.

Jack Shrimpton, the highwayman, was a native of Penn, and his local knowledge proved so useful that 'he did always the most damage between London and Oxford, insomuch that scarce a coach or horseman could pass him without being robbed'.

In the hills west of Penn are many beautiful beechwoods and remote hamlets almost untouched by time.

Ellwood's farmhouse, on Hungry Hill, now called Ongar Hill, where he held the monthly meeting of Friends for more than forty years, has been rebuilt, but the surroundings are almost unchanged. In those days Hungry Hill and the neighbouring Coleshill were in a detached portion of Hertfordshire, which made it unusually safe for Quaker meetings, as

Buckinghamshire warrants could not be executed, and the
Hertfordshire magistrates seldom thought it worth while to
send a force there. It was transferred to Buckinghamshire in
1832.

Coleshill, on high ground beyond Ongar Hill, commands
wide views over the Chilterns and has some fine old houses.
Stocks Farm, the ancient manor of the Brudenells, which
dates from the sixteenth century, was the birthplace of
Edmund Waller. The house stands in the centre of the village, and near it is an ancient oak-tree known as Waller's
Oak. A local tradition tells that the poet used to sit in the
hollow of the tree and write his verses.

iii

Eastward from Beaconsfield, along the road to London,
passing the lane to Jordans, is the wide common of Gerrards
Cross, where gorse and beech-trees run riot. Sheahan described Gerrards Cross in 1862 as 'a highly respectable place
with many genteel residences', and in spite of considerable
development north and south of the common, the description remains true to-day.

The older houses border the Common—none very old,
but with all the charm of good proportions and mantling
climbing plants. The curious church with its dome and
campanile was built by two sisters in 1859 in memory of
their brother. Its architect, Sir William Tite, who also designed the Royal Exchange, received much praise from his
contemporaries for this departure from precedent in church
design. A nearby house, the Ranche, was for many years the
home of Captain Mayne Reid, who returned to this country
after an adventurous life and wrote those thrilling stories for
boys *The Scalp Hunters*, *The Young Voyagers*, *The Boy
Hunters*, and others equally popular. Unfortunately, building speculations at Gerrards Cross involved him in financial
difficulties, and he returned to America in 1867.

One of the gates of Bulstrode Park stands at the south-west corner of the Common. The drive runs for a mile or more through the park which has existed for over 1,000 years. There is not an acre of level ground in all the 800 it covers, and it won unstinted praise from Arthur Young, who thought it one of the finest he had ever visited; and this beauty, instead of being preserved, has been cut up for building development. It is true some of it remains, but its glory has largely departed in the curtailment of its vast extent.

In the park there is an ancient British hill fort, of unusual size, with double entrenchments on the north-east and treble at some points, enclosing an area of twenty-one acres.

The early history of Bulstrode is largely traditional, a popular story telling that the Saxon owner, called Shobington, routed the forces of the Norman knight sent to dispossess him by charging them with his followers mounted on bulls. William the Conqueror sent for the rebel, who appeared at Court with his seven sons riding on bulls, and vowed fealty to the Conqueror on being confirmed in the possession of his lands, from which time the estate and its lords took the name of Bulstrode. By 1276 it was in the possession of the Knights Templars, and after their suppression in 1308 it was granted to a succession of owners.

It is not clear when or how the Bulstrodes again lived in their ancient home, but they appear to have been there for a while after the Dissolution, as Sir James Whitelocke married Elizabeth, daughter of Edward Bulstrode of 'Hedgerley Bulstrode', from whom his more famous son, Bulstrode Whitelocke of Fawley Court, derived his name. The notorious Judge Jeffreys bought the estate in 1686, and his son-in-law sold it to William Bentinck, first Earl of Portland, the devoted friend of William of Orange, who after the King's death in 1703 lived chiefly at Bulstrode.

Horace Walpole, who rode over there from Chalfont St. Peter, has little but criticism of the house and its owners, but Mrs. Montagu, when staying there during the time of the second Duke of Portland, wrote in 1741, 'I need not tell you I am very happy here; you know the persons that compose this society, and my regard for them, too well to doubt of it; . . . Bulstrode is much improved without doors; peace, cheerfulness and joy were always within; so that new furniture and fine pictures hardly make an addition to its former charms.'

The fascinating Duchess of Portland made Bulstrode a social centre, and a storehouse of beautiful works of art. Its pictures were famous—even Horace Walpole approved of those—and among its treasures was the famous Portland Vase, now in the British Museum. In the garden were many rare flowers, and 'every English plant in a separate garden by themselves', wrote Mrs. Lybbe Powys when on a visit in 1769. There were great aviaries with large and small birds from all parts of the world, and a menagerie of which Mrs. Montagu said, 'The Duchess of Portland is as eager in collecting animals, as if she foresaw another deluge, and was assembling every creature after its kind, to preserve the species.' Incidentally her husband is said to have had the curious distinction of being robbed by Dick Turpin in his own park!

The brilliant gatherings of statesmen were continued under the rule of the third Duke, who was twice Prime Minister, but after his death there in 1809, it was sold to the Duke of Somerset, by whom the present house was built in 1855, on the site of the older mansion. The estate was sold for building development in 1932.

Bulstrode Park, once an outlying portion of the parish of Upton-cum-Chalvey, in whose old church some of the Bulstrodes are commemorated with interesting brasses, is now in the parish of Hedgerley, and there is a walk through the park to the peaceful valley in which the village of Hedgerley lies, to the south of the great estate.

Hedgerley church, although modern, and not even marking the site of the original church, is disarmingly picturesquely set on a grassy hill above the little hamlet. There are some good brasses brought from the older church, including a palimpsest to Margaret Bulstrode, who died in 1540, and her ten sons and three daughters. The font has Tudor roses and small reliefs of faces cut in the fifteenth century, on a twelfth-century bowl. In the tower there is a curious seventeenth-century painting of the Commandments, but the pride of the church is a piece of red velvet, now in a frame on the south wall of the chancel, which is traditionally said to be part of a cloak given by Charles II for an altar frontal, when he saw the poverty-stricken appearance of the church in his day. The satinwood pulpit, reading-desk, and two chairs were brought from Antigua in 1843, after the church in which they stood was destroyed by an earthquake.

Although mid-way between the London to Oxford highway and the Great West Road, Hedgerley is like a survival from the past. Only the seventeenth-century Shell House has any pretensions to architectural interest, and its charm lies in its situation in a typical Chiltern 'bottom', in a clearing among the woods.

HIGH WYCOMBE, or Chipping Wycombe, as it used to be called, is now a hive of industry, second only to Slough in size, and bearing little trace in its buildings of the town which so captivated William Camden in the sixteenth century, but still meriting his commendation: 'This towne for faire building is equall to the greatest townes of this shire', so far as the centre of the town is concerned. The housing estates which have for ever spoiled the beauty of its setting of hills are a different matter.

The High Street itself has altered but little since the eighteenth century, when the charming Guildhall and the octagonal market hall were built, and the houses on the south side of White Hart Street and the west of Church Street are nearly all of sixteenth-century work, refronted with brick.

The parish church is the largest in the county. Some of the architectural details are interesting, and there are sixteenth- and seventeenth-century brasses; a seventeenth-century monument to Jacob Wheeler, a shoemaker, has cobblers' tools on it; several eighteenth-century sculptures, including a huge monument to the first Earl of Shelburne, by Peter Scheemakers; and a rather charming epitaph to a lady who 'preferred to be, rather than seem, learned'. Some curious inscriptions are to be found in the churchyard.

High Wycombe has been a place of importance since the earliest times. The district abounds in British pile-dwellings, earthworks, and remains, of which the most important is Desborough Castle, popularly called 'the Roundabout', a mile westward. There are also many traces of Roman occupation, including some fine tessellated pavements in Penn Mead. Anglo-Saxon remains, including personal ornaments, have been dug up in the neighbourhood, and the Norman period is marked by the remains of a Priory, the traces of Norman work in the parish church, and the site of the Norman castle.

Although there is no mention of Wycombe as a borough in Domesday Book, it was certainly incorporated by the reign of Henry II at latest. The cloth industry was referred to in 1221, when a tithe of teasels was recorded. There is mention of the burgesses of Wycombe as an hereditary class as early as 1185, and their most ancient privilege was the right to common pasture for two cows and a heifer on the meadow called the Rye, a privilege they still enjoy.

The earliest officers of the borough were the bailiffs, but there has been a mayor in office since the reign of Edward I. A unique ceremony takes place in connection with the annual election. Directly after he has been appointed, the Mayor is conducted to a weighing machine, and weighed, in full view of the public, in his regalia of office. The origin and significance of the ceremony are unknown, but it has undoubtedly taken place for centuries.

The borough also had an unbroken record of representation in Parliament by two members from 1300 to the Reform Act of 1832, which deprived it of one member. Later it was deprived of representation, but in the present century has regained the right to return a member to Parliament.

In a town with such a long existence there is, of course, a wealth of history to be unearthed by those who are interested, and the *History and Antiquities of Wycombe* by John Parker makes fascinating reading. Not the least interesting is the record of lace-making in the town and neighbourhood, for which Buckinghamshire was once famous. The chair-making industry, which developed in the beechwoods of the Chilterns in the eighteenth century, is still the principal industry of the town, and although the greater part of the work is now done in factories, it is still possible to find the 'chair-bodgers' turning the parts of a chair on their primitive pole-lathes in the Chiltern woods; and it is well worth while to seek them out, and watch their skilled work in the lovely forest glades.

William Cobbett, who rode through the town in 1822, said, 'High Wycombe, as if the name was ironical, lies along the bottom of a narrow and deep valley, the hills on each side being very steep indeed. The valley runs somewhere about from east to west. . . . Wycombe is a very fine and very clean market town; the people all looking extremely well; the girls somewhat larger featured and larger boned than those in Sussex, and not so fresh-coloured and bright-eyed. More like the girls of America, and that is saying quite as much as any reasonable woman can expect or wish for.'

Ten years after his visit Disraeli was at Wycombe can-vassing for his first election as Member for the Borough. He described his dramatic appeal in a letter to his friend Mrs. Austen: 'All Wycombe was assembled. Feeling it was the crisis, I jumped up on the portico of the Red Lion and gave it them for an hour and a quarter. I can give you no idea of the effect. I made them all mad. A great many absolutely *cried*. I never made as many friends in my life or converted as many enemies. All the women are on my side and wear my colours, pink and white. . . .' There is a life-sized Red Lion on the portico of the inn which, incidentally, belonged for centuries to Brasenose College, Oxford—and a local tra-dition tells that Disraeli pointed to its head, saying, 'When the poll is declared, I shall be there', adding, as he pointed to the tail, 'and my opponent will be there'. Unfortunately for Disraeli, he was no true prophet, and his opponent won the day, but when Disraeli was returned for Maidstone five years later the citizens of High Wycombe subscribed for illuminations in his honour!

Like all Buckinghamshire towns, High Wycombe was a stronghold of Dissent, in spite of the fact that it supported the Royalists during the Civil War. Wesley has many references to the town in his *Journal*, and Hannah Ball, who lived in High Wycombe for the greater part of her life, came under his influence. She opened one of the earliest Sunday schools in the kingdom at High Wycombe in 1769.

A bridge over the little River Wye, just beyond the handsome modern buildings of the Civic Centre, leads to Wycombe Abbey, originally built in 1795, on the site of Lord Shelburne's mansion, Loakes. Wesley walked through the grounds in 1775, and described them in his *Journal*. Dr. Johnson, who stayed there two days in 1783, during the absence of the owner, also praised it. Other notable visitors were the Abbé Morellet and Benjamin Franklin.

The building was never an abbey, and has no history. It was opened as a school in 1896, since when it has become one of the most famous girls' schools in the country.

West Wycombe, two and a half miles from High Wycombe, is a complete contrast to that busy, thriving town. Its long village street, almost entirely of seventeenth- and eighteenth-century buildings, is set in the rolling hills of the Chilterns, and dominated by the church and manor-house with which all its history is bound up. The influence of the wealthy, cultured Dashwoods preserved the old-world charm of the village until changing conditions threatened its beauty, but the Royal Society of Arts stepped in, and purchased the entire village in 1929. It was handed over to the National Trust five years later, and in 1943 the house with its 300 acres of grounds was handed over to the Trust by Sir John Dashwood.

Church and mausoleum are set 600 feet above the village, and the path up is so steep that all who know Arthur Young's complaint, 'Was St. Paul to preach in this Church, he must furnish the neighbours with more than mortal legs to become his auditors', are likely to echo his sentiments.

John Wilkes may have been right in thinking Sir Francis Dashwood built the church for a prospect, but he at least had the excuse that a church had stood on the same site from Norman times. Traces of thirteenth- and fourteenth-century work still survive, but in 1763 the eccentric lord of the manor, then Lord le Despencer, destroyed its whole character, removing the arcades, and turning the nave into a resemblance to a Classical drawing-room, with comfortable armchairs doing duty for pulpit and reading-desk, exquisite paintings and stucco decorations on the ceiling and walls, and a marble floor. Some brasses and monuments from the original church were also preserved.

Strangest feature of all is the golden ball surmounting the tower, the top of which is 100 feet above the ground. It is sufficiently large to hold ten or twelve people and, having been built by the eccentric founder of the Knights of St. Francis at Medmenham, it goes without saying queer tales are told of the doings in that confined space!

The fortifications which defended the British village can be seen running parallel with the churchyard fence, and near the eastern gate is the mausoleum containing memorials to members of the Dashwood family and their friends. There is a cave in the hillside below which is also said to have seen the strange meetings of the 'Knights'.

West Wycombe Park stands on a hill on the opposite side of the valley. The double colonnade designed by Robert Adam is the finest of the four façades.

ii

The little River Wye, which rises near West Wycombe, flows through the grounds of West Wycombe Park, but soon leaves these solitudes for a succession of towns and residential centres—High Wycombe, which it skirts on the south, Loudwater, a modern residential area which is increasing so rapidly it will soon reach High Wycombe, and

down to Wooburn, which, with Wooburn Green, fills the
rest of the valley down to Bourne End and the Thames.
Both Wooburn and Wooburn Green have a number of old-
world cottages, especially attractive where they are grouped
round the large oval Green. The old Royal Oak Inn, now a
private house, has two seventeenth-century carved wooden
figures.

The parish church of Wooburn has been so much altered
that it is practically new, and the elaborate screen, ablaze
with red, blue, green, and gold, dates from 1899, yet there is
still some late Norman work to tell of its early foundation,
and some good early brasses and inscriptions.

Wooburn Green was at one time known as Bishop's
Wooburn, from a manor-house of the Bishops of Lincoln,
with whom it was a favourite residence in the sixteenth
century. Bishop Atwater died there in 1521, and Bishop
Longland, confessor to Henry VIII, in 1547. It passed to the
Goodwins in the sixteenth century, one of whom was a
friend of John Hampden. He helped to organize the demon-
stration of local freeholders, who marched to London to
protect Hampden when he was in danger of arrest. His
daughter, Jane, was the second wife of Philip, the fourth
Lord Wharton, who in his eighty-three years of life was a
friend of Cromwell, a supporter of the Presbyterians, and
lived to invite William of Orange to the English throne.
He had a taste for architecture and gardening, and is said to
have spent £30,000 in pulling down the old bishop's palace
and replacing it with a magnificent mansion, in which he
entertained William III. He is best remembered in the
present day for the annual distribution of bibles and cate-
chisms to children in villages on his estates in Buckingham,
Yorkshire, Westmorland, and Cumberland.

The 'good' Lord Wharton was succeeded by his son,
whose contemptible character was described in a biting
satirical poem by Pope as 'the scorn and wonder of our

days'. His son, created Duke of Wharton, much resembled him, and eventually died in exile and poverty abroad.

The moat and fishponds of the old episcopal palace can still be seen, but the mansion has followed the earlier building into oblivion, with the exception of one of the stable wings, new fronted and turned into the present Wooburn House, which is sheltered by Lombardy poplars planted in 1777, and has an ancient entrance lodge.

iii

In the lovely, remote district which lies between the valley of the Wye and the Oxfordshire border is a tangle of country lanes threading narrow valleys, or climbing steeply to the hill-tops which command such wonderful views over this beautiful corner of the Chilterns. It is a district full of 'Ends', in the old Buckinghamshire sense of the word. Lane End and Cadmore End have felt the blight of progress, but when they are left behind there is nothing to distract the eye from delighting in the perfect mating of natural scenery and architectural beauty of which our ancestors held the secret.

Here, too, the traditional customs have died hard, and the last representative of the local Mummers survived at Wheeler End until 1933. The Buckinghamshire dialect is still natural to the older generation. All who cherish the old speech and ways must feel a debt of gratitude to Mr. H. Harman, who has preserved them in his books *Bucks Dialect* and *Sketches of the Bucks Countryside*, which re-people these old hamlets and make them live again for us.

In these lanes, worn deep by the passing of countless generations back at least to Saxon times, and most probably to the days of the ancient Britons, three places are outstanding: Fingest, Turville, and Ibstone.

Fingest, in all its perfection of grouping, lies at the head of the long Hambleden valley rising up from the Thames, with a strikingly picturesque Norman tower capped by a thirteenth-century double-packsaddle roof. On the north of the churchyard is the site of the palace of the Bishops of Lincoln, who held the manor until 1547. There is a tradition that in 1330 Bishop Henry de Burghersh enclosed some of the common lands in his park, and after his death in 1343 he appeared to one of his gentlemen clad as a huntsman in a green tunic, with bow and arrows and horn, and told him that his enclosure had given offence to God by its injustice to the poor. As a punishment, he had been put in charge of the park until the enclosed land was restored to its own possessors, and he begged his squire to see that restitution was made. Brother Thomas Walsingham of the Abbey of St. Albans, who recorded the incident, also records that the restitution was duly made.

Turville, in the next valley, forms another lovely picture, with dormered cottages round a little green and a great windmill on the hillside above. There is an eighteenth-century mansion on the west of the village, where General Dumouriez died in 1823, after having received a pension for acting as adviser to the War Office in the struggle against Napoleon. Between 1840 and 1854 it was the home of Lord Chancellor Lyndhurst, son of the American artist John Copley, whose last speech in Parliament, at the age of eighty-nine, showed no diminution in his brilliance, which was equalled by the sweetness and vivacity of his disposition throughout his long life. There is a well at the house dated 1308, and a public road across the park, shaded by a beautiful lime avenue.

Turville Court was built in 1847 on an older site, and part of the estate at one time belonged to Bysshe Shelley, grandfather of the poet.

The nave of the little church, with its low sixteenth-century tower, dates from the twelfth century. It is an attractive example of a village church, set beside the green, and backed by fine trees. There is a thought-provoking

Friends Meeting House, Jordans

Old Almshouses, Quainton

D'Oyley Tomb, Hambleden Church

CHRISTVS MIHI VITA ET MORS MIHI LVCRVM AD PHILIP CAT

Lady Lee's Tomb, Aylesbury Church

mystery in connexion with the coffin, which originally contained the body of a thirteenth-century priest, but which, when opened in modern times, was found to contain the skeleton of a woman with a bullet-mark on one of her bones, who had been buried 'in woollen' presumably in accordance with the Act passed at the end of the seventeenth century to aid the wool trade.

The road which climbs steeply uphill from Turville to Ibstone gives a fine view of Fingest and the Hambleden valley, and for the last part of the way runs along the summit of the ridge, giving wide views on either hand. Ibstone church is extremely isolated and quite unspoiled. It was transferred from Oxfordshire to Bucks in 1895, and stands about a mile to the south-west of the scattered village. It is a delightful little building with much Norman work and stands on a steep and beautifully wooded slope. It has a very well-proportioned, spacious interior for so small a building, with a high Norman chancel arch, and a carved wooden pulpit dating from the fifteenth century. In the churchyard is a large and ancient yew-tree, unusually set on the north-west of the church, and a broken stone coffin. Close by is the seventeenth-century Manor House Farm, which belongs to Merton College, Oxford; and Ibstone House, of eighteenth-century work, standing 500 feet above sea-level.

A good road continues along the ridge northward to join the main Oxford road a little west of Stokenchurch, another village which was transferred from Oxfordshire in the nineteenth century It is on one of the highest points of the Chiltern Hills, and although the main road runs through the village, it contrives to remain the village of tradition, with its old houses, duck-pond, ancient church, eighteenth-century inn, and village green. Its elevation has drawbacks, for the parish is liable to drought, and the well was dug about 1870, after a water famine when beer was cheaper than water!

The church has a considerable amount of Norman and later work, two good early fifteenth-century brasses, and later brasses to the Tipping family. Hannah Ball, the friend of John Wesley, was buried at Stokenchurch.

High Wycombe lies seven miles eastward along the main road, and a mile and a half north from the town is Hughenden, to which a visit is almost obligatory to every visitor to High Wycombe. Who does not know of Disraeli's associations with Hughenden? Even those who do not care to read of historical events have been familiarized with the outstanding moments in the career of England's most flamboyant Prime Minister by the film in which George Arliss so brilliantly interpreted his fascinating and complex character.

The site of the old manor-house of Hughenden is marked by the nineteenth-century farm-house of Rockhalls, which has five stone shields from the old house built into its walls, and old paintings, on panels, discovered recently in an upper room. Only a small part of the present Hughenden Manor is ancient, and its interest dates from its purchase by Disraeli in 1847. The church, which stands in the beautiful park, has been almost entirely rebuilt, but there are a few traces of earlier work, and a fine series of tombs which have the curious distinction of being forgeries perpetrated by a local family, the Wellbournes, in the Tudor period, in an effort to make out a connexion with the great family of de Montfort! Only the effigy of a knight in fourteenth-century plate armour is genuine. A horrifying effigy of an emaciated figure in a shroud with a small figure on its breast representing the departing spirit, dates from the sixteenth century or earlier. There is a mural with a medallion of Disraeli in profile and an affectionate inscription from Queen Victoria, near the seat in which he used to sit. His grave is in the churchyard, where he lies with his beloved wife, and near his brothers, Ralph and James. A large part of the park is in the care of the National Trust, and some of the rooms in the Manor are open to the public, with relics and personal belongings of the great statesman preserved there.

Disraeli spent his youth at Bradenham Manor, a fine mansion in which the third Lord Windsor had entertained Queen Elizabeth, but which had been much altered in the eighteenth century. It lies in the hills north-west of Hughenden, beside the road to Princes Risborough. It was Isaac D'Israeli's friendship with Pye, the Poet Laureate, which led him into Bucks. He lived at Bradenham from 1829 until his death in 1848, and is buried in the church. His son, Benjamin, described Bradenham under the name of 'Hurstley' in his novel *Endymion*, which reflects the deep love he had for the home of his boyhood.

The small church has a Norman south door, interesting memorials and two of the five surviving bells of Michael de Wymbis, dating from about 1300.

Two sections of Grim's Dyke, each about 500 yards long, can be traced north of the village.

CHAPTER TEN: *The Upper and Lower Icknield Way*

THE Icknield Way is one of the oldest roads in Buckinghamshire. It originally ran from the coast of Norfolk to the coast of Hampshire, and great portions are still easily traceable, particularly in its journey across Bucks. It splits into the Upper and Lower Icknield Way soon after entering the county on the north-east, at Edlesborough, which do not reunite until after they have left the county near Bledlow, on the south-west. The Upper Road, as its name implies, follows the northern edge of the Chilterns, and the Lower Road skirts the foot of the escarpment, along the southern edge of the Vale of Aylesbury.

Speculation on the origin of the road has been both ingenious and contradictory for at least 300 years, but one thing is clear—the road was in existence before the time of the Romans. It may be one of the four chief roads of Britain, mentioned in old Welsh laws, and described by Geoffrey of Monmouth, who says King Belinus caused them to be made, and was especially careful to proclaim that 'the cities and the highways that led unto the city should have the same peace that Dunwallo had established therein'. A record made by King Eadweard in 903 mentioned the 'Icenhylte' as the boundary of some land as far as 'the heathen burials'.

The Icknield Way enters Buckinghamshire in a lonely region commanding vast sweeps of the Chiltern Hills and the Vale to the north, with the ancient cultivation terraces or lynchets on the hillsides still clearly marked, and many of them still cultivated.

The track is some 500 feet above sea level as it enters the county, with the steep slopes above it dotted with juniper, yew, and occasional bushes of box. The Way itself is edged with the significantly named traveller's joy and wayfaring tree, with the splendidly placed church of Edlesborough as a landmark for many miles.

The village lies under the bare slopes of the Chilterns, with a large open green bordered with old brick-and-timber cottages, and the church on a hillock at the western end. It is a notably fine medieval church, with good proportions and unusually rich fittings, including a magnificently carved pulpit with a tall canopy, rood-screen, and carved stalls, two good sixteenth-century brasses, effigies dating from 1592, and some remarkable corbels on the east wall.

Henry John Todd, the editor of Milton, and himself the author of numerous religious works, was rector of Edlesborough from 1805 to 1807. His new and enlarged edition of Dr. Johnson's *Dictionary* was said by Lipscombe to be 'a lasting monument of his taste, learning, and erudition'.

There are a number of moated houses, including Manor Farm and Butler's Farm, and an old windmill, which the road passes on its way to the point near Ivinghoe, where the road forks into the Upper and Lower Way. It is probably one of the oldest remaining post mills in England, and is now in the care of the National Trust.

Ivinghoe Beacon, which rises to nearly 800 feet above sea level, is one of the highest peaks of the Chiltern Hills. It was probably here, above 'the slumbering Midland plain' that Rupert Brooke wrote his poem *The Chilterns*. The ancient and charming little town lies considerably to the west, on the lower slopes of the Ivinghoe Hills. Once a place of considerable importance, it is now a haunt of those who love the by-ways where the spirit of the past still lingers. Its hospitable inn, although altered and modernized, has many traces of the original fifteenth-century building. There are a number of old houses, a sixteenth-century Town Hall, and a splendid church, so fine as to be almost a cathedral.

The Manor of Ivinghoe was a possession of the See of

Winchester from Saxon times until the reign of Henry VIII,
and the church owes its striking architecture to the bishops.
Originally built about 1230, it is now mostly of the Decorated period. The fifteenth-century wooden roofs are
lavishly ornamented with carved figures of angels holding
shields, and other decorative work. The capitals of the pillars
beautifully carved with stiff leaved foliage, the quaint
fifteenth-century poppy-head carving of the pew-ends, the
seventeenth-century pulpit with its large hour-glass stand
and elaborately carved canopy; the amusing corbels; many
brasses, suspected of having their inscriptions mixed; an
unusually large thatch-hook hanging on the wall—all go to
make up a notable display for the eager visitor.

It was from Ivinghoe that Sir Walter Scott evolved the
name of his famous novel *Ivanhoe*, choosing it for its 'ancient
English sound', in the rhyme quoted on page 74. Other
rhymes on Tring, Wing, and Ivinghoe mention these
attractive places unflatteringly, for no discernible reason.

There are widespreading views from the Ivinghoe Hills
and Ivinghoe Common, which are part of the 3,370 acres of
wood, heath, and downland on the Ashridge estate now in
the care of the National Trust, and there is an indicator on
the summit of Beacon Hill showing the principal places of
interest visible.

Pitstone church stands apart from its village, in treeless
upland fields backed by Pitstone Hill, which rises to 700 feet.
The earliest work in the church dates from about 1250, but
there is a beautiful font, and some carved fragments dating
from a century earlier. The attractive interior has an enormous and elaborately carved pulpit, old benches, a box pew,
carved capitals, old tiles on the chancel floor, an early medieval chest of unusual design, and other interesting details.

Church Farm incorporates the ancient Pitstone Place, and
has a homestead moat. Ashridge House, an early nineteenth-
century mansion on the site of a famous convent of the Bon-

hommes founded by Prince Edward, brother of Henry III, stands in a spacious park bordering the parish. It was included in Buckinghamshire until the nineteenth century, when it was transferred to Hertfordshire.

Half a mile past the lane down to Pitstone church, the Upper Icknield Way marks the boundary between Buckinghamshire and Hertfordshire until it reaches the bridge over the Grand Junction Canal. The narrow tongue of Hertfordshire which thrusts northward into Bucks is only two miles wide, and Buckinghamshire is regained just before the Icknield Way is crossed by Roman Akeman Street, now a part of the modern highway to Aylesbury. The older road follows Akeman Street for a short distance before striking out again on its way—and a very lonely way, too, although sufficiently modernized to be a winding country lane without the old grass borders which are characteristic of the untouched original Way. At Halton it is represented by the modern road running through the park at the back of Halton House, which was formerly a mansion of the Rothschilds, and is now part of the R.A.F. Camp. Halton church, built in 1813, has a sixteenth-century brass to Henry Bradshawe, Chief Baron of the Exchequer.

There is a tradition that it was in the woods of Halton that Sir Adam de Gurdon, who was dispossessed of his estates for siding with de Montfort in the Barons' War, fought with Edward I in single combat, with such valour that, although defeated, he won the King's admiration and life-long friendship.

Beyond Halton Woods the hills recede, and the road and railway from Aylesbury to London make their way through a gap between Boddington Hill and Bacombe Hill, with the Icknield Way running through Wendover as High Street and Pound Street.

Wendover's name alone is sufficient indication of its antiquity. Although *The Place-names of Buckinghamshire* by

A. Mawer and F. M. Stenton says non-committally, 'Probably an old stream-name', Wendover in its modern form is sufficiently akin to the Welsh 'gwyn dwfr'—white or bright water—to show its British origin.

Beautifully set in a fold of the Chilterns, Wendover displays the good sense of so many little Buckinghamshire towns in preserving the older part intact and developing the new suburb on its outskirts. Wendover was anciently a place of some importance, and not only had a market from an early period, but was granted the right to hold a yearly fair as early as 1214. The borough returned two burgesses to Parliament in the early fourteenth century, but allowed the privilege to lapse until 1625. It was then the smallest borough in England, but had a remarkably distinguished list of representatives, including John Hampden, Richard Steele, Edmund Burke, and George Canning. Wendover was for many years the pocket borough of the Earls Verney. Corruption was rife, and the constables of the borough worked openly to return the candidates brought forward by the lord of the manor, until the passing of the Reform Bill.

Although the Market Hall is modern, and some of the shop-fronts in the High Street have been greatly altered, the town as a whole has many picturesque brick-and-timber houses, and even a few thatched cottages. The fine old inns include the Red Lion, where R. L. Stevenson stayed in 1875, and recorded his appreciation in *An Autumn Effect*: 'I never saw any room much more to. be admired than the low wainscoted parlour in which I spent the remainder of the evening'. He was not so appreciative of the town itself, and does less than justice to the wide main street with its attractive old houses and its views of hill and vale.

Wendover church and manor-house, nearly half a mile away, are reached by a pretty path beside a little stream. They may mark the original settlement.

Wendover church was of great local importance in the

Middle Ages, its rood-cross being a place of pilgrimage. In 1506 people at Chesham, who had spoken against idolatry and superstition, were sentenced to make a pilgrimage to the cross. The rood-screen was taken down in 1842.

The church is chiefly of Decorated work, although it has a Norman font from an earlier church on the site. There are quaint carvings on the unusual piers of the chancel. Among the brasses is one to William Bradshawe, who died in 1539, with his wife and nine children, which also names twenty-three grand-children. The lengthy epitaph to Henry Brad-shawe, who died in 1674, says:

> 'Three things he priz'd contemning earthly pelf
> To God, his duty, neighbour, and himself.
> His Charity was great, his Mercy good,
> He cloath'd the naked, gave the hungry food,
> The Tomb's no grave unto the just
> But a receptacle of their dust.'

Three famous men were born in Wendover: Roger de Wendover, the chronicler and monk of St. Albans, who died in 1236, to whose *Flowers of History* Walsingham said the chroniclers of England owe nearly everything; Richard of Wendover, Bishop of Rochester, who died in 1250, and another Richard of Wendover, the great physician. He was a Canon of St. Paul's and author of many valuable writings on medical subjects, and died in 1252. The first Savings Bank in England was established at Wendover in 1799 by the Rev. Joseph Smith.

Wendover is a deservedly popular centre for exploring the Chiltern Hills and Vale of Aylesbury. Coombe Hill, rising to 850 feet, is the highest hill of the Buckinghamshire Chilterns, and a splendid viewpoint. The summit is marked by a monument on which 148 names are inscribed in memory of soldiers who fell in the Boer War.

Chequers Court, presented to the nation by Lord Lee of

Fareham in 1917, is the country home of the Prime Ministers of England. It lies two and a half miles south-west of Wendover, in a shallow dip of the wooded hills. Built on the site of an older house in the sixteenth century, it has been restored to its original character in the present century. The history of Chequers goes back some 700 years, and it has associations with descendants of Cromwell through an intricate series of marriages.

The Icknield Way, made into a modern highway, runs south-west from Wendover to Princes Risborough, through typical Chiltern scenery. The tower of Ellesborough church comes into sight as the Way switchbacks to Butler's Cross, where a road from Aylesbury to the Hampdens crosses it. Built of flint, on an ancient tumulus, this Perpendicular church is splendidly placed on a spur of the northern Chilterns. There is a portrait brass with an inscription to Thomas Hawtrey, who died in 1544. He was a member of the family who built Chequers Court. Another Hawtrey, Brigetta, who was the wife of Sir H. Croke, and died in 1638, has a magnificent monument with a graceful effigy. There is also a tablet to Sir John Russell, a descendant of Cromwell's daughter, Frances, by her marriage to an earlier Sir John Russell. In the churchyard is the grave of Thomas Edwards, who figures in Nichol's *Literary Anecdotes* and is chiefly remembered for his quarrel with Bishop Warburton. He lived at Terrick, in Ellesborough parish, for the last seventeen years of his life.

The district is full of delightful by-ways, some of which run through the great park of Chequers, whose trees shade the Icknield Way on its journey to Little Kimble and its diminutive church, which has some ancient glass, good woodwork, a Norman font, six thirteenth-century tiles representing scenes from the story of Tristram and Iseult, and some exceptionally fine fourteenth-century mural paintings. In the churchyard is a monument to Stephen

Quartermaine, who died in 1831, with an inscription claiming that he was a 'descendant of the ancient family of Quartremains of Oxfordshire, once the possessors of Sherborne Castle'. Two elm-trees in the churchyard have grown together in a curious way.

Great Kimble church is barely a quarter of a mile from Little Kimble. It was here, in January 1635, that John Hampden refused to pay ship-money and precipitated the war which gave Parliament the ascendancy over the monarchy.

The Decorated church has been ruthlessly restored, but has a fine Norman font. A large tumulus behind the church was opened in 1887, and found to contain prehistoric relics. Pulpit hill, in Chequers Park, has a great Camp said to have been the site of the fortress of the British chieftain Cunobelinus—Shakespeare's *Cymbeline*—from whom the villages of Great and Little Kimble traditionally derive their name.

George Surnnock, who was presented to the living of Great Kimble in 1660 by John Hampden's son, Richard, was speedily ejected for his Nonconformist sympathies, and spent the rest of his life producing a multiplicity of sermons and treatises, including *The Pastor's Farewell*, *A Valedictory Sermon Preached at Great Kimble*, 1662, still well known to collectors.

Much of the village, and all the charm of the Icknield Way, have been destroyed here by its widening into a modern motor road on its way to Princes Risborough, but about two miles short of the town it climbs the hills again and resumes its ancient character.

Monks Risborough belonged to Christ Church, Canterbury, in Saxon times, and passed into the possession of Lanfranc, Archbishop of Canterbury, at the Conquest. The remarkably fine and interesting church has a considerable amount of Perpendicular work, with some interesting brasses, a good Perpendicular rood-screen, ancient tiles, and a carved Norman font. The delightful old houses and cottages of the little village cluster near the church, and in the neighbouring meadows are some attractive old farm-buildings, and an early sixteenth-century square dovecote with an elaborately carved doorway.

Above the village towers Whiteleaf Hill, with the famous Whiteleaf Cross, cut in the turf. It is a fruitful source of speculation to antiquarians. Over 30 feet in height and 80 feet across, it is said to be visible for over 30 miles, and although some have suggested it may be of seventeenth-century origin, the balance of opinion inclines to an origin of great antiquity—at least Saxon, and possibly even of British origin. There is a local tradition that this and the Bledlow cross were regularly cleaned or 'scoured' like the White Horses of Uffington and Westbury.

The old village of Whiteleaf is on the Upper Icknield Way, but its cottages have been renovated all too successfully, and are almost hidden by fantastic bungalows and houses.

The newer part of Princes Risborough lies between the old town and the station. The old coaching town lies close to the church and the mounds of earth which mark the traditional site of the palace of the Black Prince, from which Princes Risborough derives the first part of its name. The church is so thoroughly restored that only traces of Early English work remain, but there are two good corbels, and a delicately moulded triple lancet window dating from about 1280 filled with unusually attractive Victorian stained glass. An old iron chest contains valuable Elizabethan documents.

Neighbouring the church is an interesting manor-house with fine woodwork, including a beautiful carved Jacobean staircase. It is now the property of the National Trust. The Old Vicarage has timbered walls, a tiled roof, and an unusual outside chimney, and nearby there are a number of other interesting old houses and cottages. The broad High Street has typical Georgian brick-and-half-timbered houses and cottages and a quaint little stilted Market House.

Sir Peter Lely, the Court painter, who has preserved for us the beauties of Charles II's Court and figures in Pepys' *Diary*, lived for a while in the town.

Princes Risborough is an excellent centre for exploring the north-west of the Buckinghamshire Chilterns and the Vale of Aylesbury. A steep road up to Lacey Green gives one of the best views possible of Grim's Dyke, an ancient earthwork which crossed the Chilterns, and can be traced at intervals from Bradenham to Berkhamsted. It may have been a boundary between the old Saxon Kingdoms, or of even earlier origin. Nearby is the Pink and Lily Inn, a favourite haunt of that gifted young poet, Rupert Brooke. In this neighbourhood, too, is the hamlet of Speen, whose ancient inn achieved widespread fame when Ramsay MacDonald's daughter, Ishbel, became its hostess. In a little graveyard near Speen lies Eric Gill, sculptor, writer, typographer, and philosopher.

In the hills to the south is one of the many queer placenames of Bucks—Wardrobes, which has borne the name since at least as early as 1338.

Horsenden, a mile south-west of Princes Risborough, has a small church, a group of cottages, and a mansion house built in 1810 on the site of the house which Sir John Denham garrisoned for the King during the Civil War. Lipscomb describes his association with Horsenden at length. Sir John, best remembered for his poem *Cooper's Hill*, sold the estate in 1662 to John Grubb of Great Kimble, in whose family it remained until 1841, and a number of them are buried in the church. Timothy Hall, who was rector in 1667, removed to a London church, and was one of the few who read James II's Declaration from the pulpit in 1688. Presumably as a reward, he was made Bishop of Oxford, but when he went to take possession of his see 'the Dean and Canons refused to install him, the gentry to meet him, the Vice-Chancellor and heads to take notice of him, or any Master or Bachelor to take Holy Orders from him'. After the revolution he was reduced to utter penury, and died at Hackney in 1690.

Saunderton, which lies three and a half miles from the station of that name, and only a mile from Princes Risborough station, is a pleasant little backwater, with tumuli on the hills above, and a rebuilt church which retains an ancient brass, a Norman font, some medieval tiles, and fragments of ancient woodwork in the screen.

Bledlow, right on the Oxfordshire border, is an attractive village in a delightful setting. The church is an interesting medley of periods from about 1200 onwards, with a carved Norman font, mural paintings, fragments of fourteenth-century heraldic glass, and an eighteenth-century altar-piece with dummy candlesticks. There are the remains of a fifteenth-century cross in the churchyard, which reaches to the edge of the beautiful wooded ravine known as the Lyde, with its fern-draped banks and watercress beds, fed by a stream which bubbles straight up from the hillside. An old prophecy, attributed to Mother Shipton, said:

> 'They who live and do abide
> Shall see Bledlow Church fall into the Lyde,'

but so far there seems no likelihood of this disaster. Behind the village, and just above the Icknield Way, is the Bledlow Cross, cut into the turf of Wain Hill. It is only a few feet less in size than that of Whiteleaf, and presumably of identical origin. Bledlow Ridge church, on a spur of the Chilterns, is interesting only for its magnificent situation and the beautiful views it commands. The Upper Icknield Way leaves the county at the Leather Bottle Inn on the Oxfordshire boundary where there are wide views over the level pastures lying northward.

ii

The Lower Icknield Way sets out from Ivinghoe as a rather dull and straight road. It reaches the narrow upthrust of Hertfordshire a little south of Marsworth, a village on the Grand Junction Canal. The church combines Early English and Perpendicular work, and has some remarkable brasses. Mary West, who died in 1606, is shown with a chrysom child. An elaborate altar tomb to Edmund West, who died in 1618, has a brass with a curious deathbed scene, and is signed by Epiphanius Evesham, who was known to his contemporaries as 'that most exquisite Master', and whose work is more often found in Kent. Soon after the Icknield Way reaches Bucks again it passes close to a group of villages, and the road has some of its ancient character. Drayton Beauchamp, a small village, has a secluded church, standing a little apart, which is well worth a visit, not only for its monuments, but also for its association with Richard Hooker. There is fifteenth-century glass in the Perpendicular east window, depicting ten of the twelve apostles, and some fourteenth-century armorial glass. There are two unusually large and interesting brasses, one of which is to Thomas Cheyne, the shield-bearer of Edward III, and a magnificent monument to Lord Newhaven, who died in 1728, with his widow watching over him and so vividly depicted that her figure has an actual illusion of life.

Although Hooker was only rector for a year, Izaak Walton's description of a visit paid to him by his former pupils, George Cranmer and Edwin Sandys, who found him reading Horace, and minding sheep at the behest of his exacting wife, and later meekly performing household tasks, gives interest to even such a short sojourn. It was as a result of this visit that Sandys induced his father, the Archbishop of York, to bestow on the brilliant scholar and future author of *Ecclesiastical Polity* the Mastership of the Temple. The Victorian pulpit in Drayton Beauchamp church was erected to his memory.

A later rector, Dr. Lockman, tutored George the Fourth, when he stayed at Turrett house nearby, as a youth, in charge of General Lake, who is buried at Aston Clinton.

Buckland, with its twisting lanes, restored medieval church, and modern bungalows shaded with elms, need not detain us. Aston Clinton, with its old houses almost lost among the new on the modern highway which follows the line of Roman Akeman Street, has a large church in a tree-shaded churchyard. Dating chiefly from the Decorated period, it has been much restored, but has memorials to the Lake family who once owned the manor-house, the most famous of whom was Viscount Lake, who captured Delhi in 1804.

Aston Clinton Park and Halton Park are separated only by a canal. The nineteenth-century mansion at Aston Clinton, marking the site of the old manor-house of the Lakes, is one of the seven mansions built for the Rothschilds within a radius of eight miles from Aylesbury. Only the one at Tring is outside Bucks.

Between Akeman Street and the main road between Aylesbury and Wendover the exact course of the Lower Icknield Way is hard to trace, and it is possible the earliest road of all was abandoned for a more convenient approach to the villages which sprang up in later centuries, but it may have run through Weston Turville by Brooke Farm, Malthouse Row, and west of the old manor-house and the Vine Inn.

Weston Turville, with its many thatched cottages and Georgian houses, is shaded with elms and beautified with orchards. The church combines every style from Norman to Perpendicular, and is both large and light. There are fragments of old glass, a fine Norman font of the Aylesbury type, a beautifully carved pulpit dating from 1567, a small brass of about 1580, parts of a fifteenth-century screen and of an eighteenth-century altar-piece with the painted figures of Moses and Aaron, used as the doors of a cupboard.

The quarterly meetings of the Quakers from a very wide area were held at Weston Turville from 1678 to 1723, in a house still standing. The minute-book, written by Thomas Ellwood, is at the headquarters of the Society of Friends. George Fox's *Journal* also has references to the meetings 'At John Brown's, of Weston, near Aylesbury'.

Crossing the Wendover road at World's End, the Lower Icknield Way runs through Little Kimble and follows an almost straight line to the Oxfordshire border, about 100 feet below the Upper Icknield Way, and at a distance varying from one to two miles north of it, bounded on the one hand by the meadows of the Vale of Aylesbury, and on the other by the Chiltern Hills, in a lonely region where only the tiniest hamlets are found.

IT is one of the charms of Aylesbury that in addition to its
delightful old inns and houses, it has street and place-names
linking up with its past history.

Aylesbury's name is derived from the Saxon 'Aegel's
burh', but it is possible there was at least a settlement there
earlier. Roman pottery and spindles have been found in the
neighbourhood of the parish church, and the *Anglo-Saxon
Chronicle* mentions it under the date A.D. 571: 'This year
Cuthulf fought with the Britons at Bedford, and took four
towns, Lenbury, Aylesbury, Benson, and Ensham.' Aylesbury's earliest known history, however, is as a Saxon burgh,
which undoubtedly had a troubled existence at first—the
Chronicle tells us that in 921, when Edward the Elder was
pushing his conquests over the Danes, they broke through
his flank by night, taking 'no little both in men and cattle
betwixt Bernewood and Aylesbury'; and doubtless there
were other disastrous occasions, but by the reign of Edward
the Confessor, Aylesbury was the centre of eight hundreds
which formed a 'circuit' paying scot to Aylesbury church.

There was a mint there from the tenth to the eleventh
century, from which coins were issued in the reigns of
Ethelred II, Canute, and Edward the Confessor.

Strangely enough, in view of its importance and its
extremely central position, Aylesbury was not made the
county town until modern times, and was not even incorporated as a borough until 1553. Nevertheless, it usurped
most of the county business. Assizes were held at Aylesbury
from 1218 onwards, and possibly earlier. The election of
knights of the shire took place at Aylesbury, and the King's
Bench moved there in 1351. The county gaol was kept there

from at least as early as 1180—though in the earlier centuries
it appears to have been more satisfactory to the prisoners
than to the authorities, for in 1276 the gaoler is said to have
allowed women to escape at one shilling a head, and in spite
of extensive repairs felons escaped in considerable numbers
up to the middle of the fourteenth century.

The ancient town was built entirely on the summit and
slopes of the hill which is still crowned by the parish church
founded by the Saxons, with Kingsbury square immediately
east of church square marking the traditional site of the residence of Saxon, Norman, and Plantagenet kings. The sixteenth-century Castle Fee and the name of Castle Street
suggest that it had defensive works, but the many references
to royal visits to the town suggest something more in the
nature of a fortified manor-house or hospicium.

Henry I and Queen Maud stayed at Aylesbury between
1100 and 1117, and in 1179 Henry II granted a messuage
known as Otters Fee, the site of which may be indicated by
the name of Otterells Lane, to his otter-hunter, Roger
Follus, for the service of supplying the King with straw for
his bed in winter, and grass for his 'hospicium' in summer,
and with two geese or three eels thrice yearly 'if the King
visited the town'.

On high ground south-west of the Market Square stood
the Franciscan friary, founded in 1386, the south-west
boundary of which is marked by the modern Friarage Road.
Foundations and stone-work have been found in the grounds
of the house known as 'the Primroses'. With the exception
of the church, all the early medieval buildings known to
have existed in the town have disappeared, but the old
King's Head is a fine specimen of a late medieval timber
house, dating back to 1450, and enjoying the unusual distinction of being the property of the National Trust whilst
still in use as an hotel. The original glass in the large window
consists of fragments of the figures of angels holding shields,

on some of which are the arms of Henry VI and his Queen, Margaret of Anjou. There is also a seventeenth-century stair-case with twisted balusters. A local tradition recounts that Cromwell slept in one of the rooms in 1651, when he received the delegates sent by Parliament to congratulate him on his victory at Worcester.

The Battle of Aylesbury was fought at Holman's Bridge in 1642, but Aylesbury was enthusiastically in favour of the cause of Parliament, and aided the militia to inflict a sound defeat on the Royalist forces. In 1818, over 200 human skeletons were found in a common grave near Holman's Bridge, believed to be the remains of those killed in the battle, and were later buried in Hardwick churchyard, four miles to the north of Aylesbury. The encounter at Holman's Bridge was by no means the last attack on the town during the Civil War, but it resisted all attempts at capture.

The picturesque Bull's Head Hotel was granted to John Litley in the fifteenth century. His successor in the sixteenth century was sued in Chancery for altering the term of his lease from twenty-one to sixty-one years. The oldest part of the present house dates from the seventeenth century. The main block was rebuilt in the eighteenth century.

On one occasion during 1874, as leader of the Opposition, Disraeli addressed the men of Aylesbury through a window of the George Inn (since rebuilt), criticizing the terms on which the Government had secured the freedom of the Malacca Straits.

A number of the old inns and houses of Aylesbury have been rebuilt, but there are still delightful old corners to reward the patient seeker, particularly in or near the Market Place. The quaintly-named Dark Lantern Inn is in Silver Street, and the Queen's Head is in the neighbouring Temple Square. There are some attractive old houses in Church Street, including the fine building in which the inter-esting Museum of the Buckinghamshire Archæological and

Natural History Society is housed. The Society celebrated its centenary in 1947. The Saracen's Head, on Rickford's Hill, the Rising Sun Inn, and a number of houses in the Oxford road, date from the seventeenth century.

The Prebendal, a large stucco-fronted house on the south-west of the church, was the home of John Wilkes after his marriage with Mary Meade. Wilkes was born at Leighton Buzzard, then in Buckinghamshire, and was educated at Aylesbury. He was returned unopposed as M.P. for Aylesbury in 1757. He loved his adopted town, and in the year of his election wrote to a friend of 'the wonderful verdure of the rich vale of Aylesbury, and the fragrance of its bean-fields in full blossom'. A small statuette of Wilkes goes with the lease of the Prebendal.

The town was made a parliamentary borough by Mary Tudor in 1553, the year in which it was first incorporated, and the right of election was exercised by the corporation alone until the charter lapsed, when the 'pot-wallopers' had it all their own way, and elections were carried out with the most barefaced corruption until the Reform Bill was passed.

Among the many celebrated men who represented Aylesbury in Parliament, apart from many of the Pakington and Verney families, were John Lyly, the dramatist, and author of *Euphues*, who was elected in 1593; Thomas Scott, who was executed as a regicide in 1660; Lord Nugent, author of *Memorials of John Hampden*, and other books, who was M.P. from 1812 until 1832 and from 1847 until his death in 1850; and Winthrop Mackworth Praed, the poet, who represented Aylesbury in Parliament from 1837 until his death in 1839, at the early age of thirty-seven. Richard Bethell, who sat for Aylesbury in 1851, was succeeded by Sir Austen Layard, who represented the town from 1852 to 1857, but is best remembered as the explorer of Nineveh and Babylon.

Aylesbury church is believed to have been founded before the end of the seventh century, and an arch in the crypt is a survival of the Saxon church. According to tradition the body of St. Osyth was buried there for forty-six years, after her martyrdom by Danes, but she appeared to a smith and told him she wished her bones to lie at Chich Priory, near Colchester, of which she had been abbess, and they were accordingly reburied there.

Presumably the Normans rebuilt the Saxon church, for there are some fragments of Norman work, and the font is one of the famous 'Aylesbury' type of decorative Norman work, but the present building dates from the early thirteenth century. The modern stained glass includes six large lights in the west window which were awarded a prize medal at the International Exhibition of 1862. The figures of St. Peter and St. Paul on the eastern wall of the chancel were carved at Oberammergau.

In the vestry are the marble effigy of a knight found in the grounds of the monastery of the Grey Friars, believed to be that of Sir Robert Lee of Hulcott, and the beautiful alabaster monument to Lady Lee, who died in 1584, and her three children, with the inscription:

'Entombed here dothe rest a worthie dame,
    Extract and born of noble house and blovd,
Her sire Lord Paget hight of worthie fame,
    Whose virtues cannot sink in the flovd
Two brethren had she Barõs of this realme,
    A knight heer freere Sir Henry Lee be hight
To whom she bare thre impes which had to name
    Jhou, Henry Mary slayne by fortunes spight,
First two beĩg young which caused ther parẽts mõe,
    The third in flower ãd prime of all her yeares.
All thre do rest within this marble stone
    By whiche the flicke'es of worldly joyes appears,

Good frẽd sticke but to strew with crimisõ flowers,
  This marble stone wherein her cindres rest.
For sure her ghost lyves with the heavẽly powers,
  And gverdon hathe of virtvovs life possest.'

It is pleasant to find that even in these busy and unsenti-
mental days fresh crimson flowers are still placed on her
tomb.

The oak wardrobe once used for storing surplices dates
from the fifteenth century. Above the vestry is a room with
a baluster window and an old fireplace, called the Priest's
Sleeping-chamber.

The Church registers, which date from 1564, contain
many references to the burial of people executed—chiefly
for stealing, and sometimes as many as four in a day. In 1644
a woman was executed for housebreaking on the same day
as her baby was baptised, and in 1752 two men were buried
after having been executed for a robbery of twenty-six
shillings and sixpence. In November 1745 an entry conjures
up a picture of alarums and excursions among the worthy
citizens, when 'this parish was sadly surprised through fear of
an immediate visit by the Hyland Rebells from whom Good
Lord deliver us'. Their prayer was answered, for the rebels
never came within miles of the town. In 1794 is the quaint
entry, 'A Welshman was buried in the Welsh language by
the Rev. Mr. W. Lloyd'.

In 1342 some of the townspeople, who were upholding
their right of common pasture, assaulted the steward of the
Countess of Ormonde, and when he took refuge in the
church, broke the doors and windows and imprisoned him
until he forgave their trespasses and swore to leave the
service of the countess.

The churchyard was at one time a popular pit for cock-
fighting, and even up to the beginning of the nineteenth
century elections were held there, with the rival candidates

addressing their audiences from the tombstones. On one occasion two soldiers were flogged there for their misdeeds.

The churchyard is peaceful enough to-day, with its fine shady trees and the old houses around. In the wall near the Prebendal is the tomb of William Smart, who was gardener to John Wilkes, with a line from Virgil inscribed on it: 'For him even the laurels, for him even the myrtles weep'.

The old town of Aylesbury lay entirely on the hill, and the low-lying ground now covered by the modern part of the town was so swampy that stone causeways had to be built across it, and it was not until it was drained in the nineteenth century that houses could be built there. Walton, originally a separate hamlet on the south, but now a part of the municipal borough, has a number of delightful seventeenth-century cottages close to the village green with its pond, and in Walton Street there are more old cottages and two seventeenth-century inns. Walton House is an eighteenth-century house, but some of its walls and outbuildings date from the seventeenth century.

The first Point-to-Point Steeplechase in England was run in 1835 from Waddesdon Windmill to a field just below Aylesbury church, and is vividly described in Fowler's *Echoes of Old Country Life*.

Aylesbury has always been famous for its duck-rearing, but the lace industry, for which it was one of the chief centres in Bucks in the seventeenth and eighteenth centuries, was superseded by silk-weaving and straw-plaiting. There are various accounts of the introduction of lace-making into England, the most generally accepted being that it was introduced by Katherine of Aragon, and carried on by immigrants from Flanders during the persecution of the Low Countries by Philip of Spain. Different districts developed different styles, and a beautiful Point ground style was evolved in Buckinghamshire, of which there are delicate specimens in the County Museum, which is housed in the old Grammar School of Aylesbury. The bobbins for winding the cotton were made of bone, wood, or metal, and often elaborately carved and inscribed with mottoes or names. There is a fine collection in the County Museum. The industry almost died out as the result of the introduction of machine-made lace, but is now being revived by associations formed to encourage the sale of hand-made lace.

Set as it is in the heart of the county, Aylesbury is by far the best centre from which to explore Buckinghamshire.

The surviving thatched cottages of Stoke Mandeville, three miles south-east of Aylesbury, are almost swamped in the ribbon development along the main road, and its old church, standing apart in the fields, has been so neglected that it has practically disintegrated. It has a very charming monument of the three children of Edmund Brudenell, Lord of the Manor in the reign of Elizabeth. Moat Farm, which still retains three sides of its moat, has an historic interest, for it was on this property that John Hampden refused to pay ship-money in 1635, and so started the train of events which led to the Civil War.

CHAPTER TWELVE: *Westward from Aylesbury to the Oxfordshire Border*

NORTH BUCKS is in every way a complete contrast to the south. The Vale of Aylesbury extends northwards from the Chiltern range in a great plain of fertile pasture-lands, broken only by abrupt little hills where the old cottages cluster around ancient churches and manor-houses, as they have done for centuries past. Were it not for the hedges planted during the eighteenth-century enclosures, it might well be Tudor Buckinghamshire—apart, of course, from the industrial centres at Bletchley, Fenny Stratford, and Wolverton.

Gone are the beech-woods of the Chilterns. In the country around Brill are great oaks surviving from the old forest of Bernwood, and such village names as Boarstall, Oakley, and Ashendon are a reminder that this was once a hunting forest of Saxon and Norman kings.

Every village and farm has its duck-pond, for this is the countryside which has been famous for duck-breeding since the earliest times. There are orchards, too, mostly of cherry-trees, for which Bucks is also famous. The great pastures are of comparatively late origin, introduced as sheep-runs during the heyday of the woollen trade. Many of them are crossed by curious, long, parallel curved ridges about 30 feet wide, and $1\frac{1}{2}$ feet high, which are a survival of the ancient method of ploughing, from the days when the Vale was largely arable land and the deep hollows between the ridges gave drainage to the clay soil.

Two miles from Aylesbury along the Thame road is Hartwell, which was held by the Lees from 1618, but is only remembered by the majority of people as the home of the French royal family from 1810 to 1814. The Queen of France died at Hartwell, and lay in state there before being taken to Sardinia for burial.

Hartwell House is an eighteenth-century reconstruction of an earlier manor-house. The splendid oak staircase has twenty-four large panelled newels, surmounted by statues of gods and heroes, and many of the rooms have fine panelling.

King Louis did not forget his English home when he returned to France. He gave £100 to be invested for the poor of Hartwell parish, and laid out an English garden at Versailles modelled upon the one then at Hartwell. He invited Sir George Lee, his landlord, to visit him at the Tuileries—but Sir George chose an unfortunate time: he presented himself just after news had arrived that Napoleon had escaped from Elba! The story of Hartwell is told in the *Ædes Hartwellianæ*, written by Captain, afterwards Admiral Smyth, at the request of Dr. John Lee, who inherited Hartwell in 1827.

Hartwell church is one of the most curious in England. It was built in 1753 in imitation of the chapter-house of York Minster, with a ceiling copied from King's College, Cambridge, and combines classical symmetry with Gothic detail. Boards with painted inscriptions record the names of those buried in the older church on the site, whose bodies now lie in the vault beneath the church.

The village is close under the wall of the park, which has huge ammonites built into it.

There is a good view of Hartwell House on the road to Stone, a name which unfortunately has a peculiar significance to all Bucks people, from the County Mental Hospital situated there, but has many far older associations. Stone was mentioned in Domesday Book, and had a number of notable lords of the manor until united with Hartwell in the seventeenth century.

Although drastically restored, the greater part of the

church dates from the twelfth century. The remarkably fine, richly carved Norman font was originally in the Berkshire church of Hampstead Norris. There is a wall tablet to Admiral Smyth, whom we met at Hartwell, and who was a gold medallist of the Royal Astronomical Society; and brasses to the Gurneys, and to Sir William Flower, who was an army doctor in the Crimean War, and later Director of the Natural History Museum, South Kensington.

Joseph Bancroft Reade, who was vicar of Stone from 1839 to 1859, when he became Vicar of Ellesborough, was a distinguished chemist, microscopist, and photographic discoverer, and was a President of the Royal Microscopical Society. His successor, James Booth, was treasurer and chairman of the Society of Arts.

There are fine views of the Chiltern Hills from Stone, and the village has some picturesque old cottages. At the next crossroads there is a choice of ways—one south to Dinton and the other north-east to Cuddington.

The entirely delightful village of Dinton, in a hollow shaded by elm- and chestnut-trees, with two old manor-houses and a remarkably interesting church, was the home of three men concerned in the death of Charles I: Simon Mayne, of Dinton Hall, Sir Richard Ingoldsby of Waldridge, and John Bigg, who was secretary to both. Bigg became a hermit after the Restoration and lived in a cave in the parish without ever changing his clothes, although he survived until 1696. One of his shoes is preserved at Dinton Hall, and another is in the Ashmolean Museum at Oxford.

Simon Mayne, who entertained Cromwell at Dinton Hall, died in the Tower after the Restoration as a signatory of the King's death-warrant, but was a patriot who had genuinely felt the necessity of ending the King's high-handed methods of government. He is buried in Dinton church. There is a mural monument to his father and mother, Simon and Coilubery Mayne.

Dinton Hall, originally built by Archbishop Warham about 1500, on a very interesting plan, has been much modernized. The cellars are said to date from the time of Edward the Confessor. Upper Waldridge, the home of Sir Richard Ingoldsby, is a picturesque example of early seventeenth-century half-timbering, now a farm.

Dinton church, approached through an archway in a row of old houses, is largely Early English, but it has one of the most richly carved Norman doorways in the kingdom. The lintel shows a very small St. Michael valiantly thrusting a cross down the throat of a very large dragon, typifying Satan, and the tympanum has two wyverns devouring fruit from a tree.

There are some beautiful brasses, the earliest to John Compton, who died in 1424, and a black marble slab to Colonel Richard Beke, who married Cromwell's much-loved niece, Lavinia Whetstone, as his first wife. There are also two long inscriptions in the churchyard worth searching for—one, to Samuel Paine, a ploughboy, who died in 1849, which tells his life-story in verse, and the other to Henry Wotton, a farmer who died in 1857, with a rhymed allegory.

North of the village is the sham Dinton Castle, built by Sir John Vanhattem, the eighteenth-century lord of the manor, on a Saxon burial-mound which has yielded interesting relics, including a beautiful Saxon drinking-glass, and numerous skeletons.

Cuddington rivals Dinton in charm, with its ochre-washed cottages round a village green above the River Thame, and a very attractive church. It is true the church cannot match the Norman doorway at Dinton, but it has an interesting blending of styles from Norman to Perpendicular. The font is Norman; there are some quaint epitaphs; two fifteenth-century angels in stained glass; and the altar rail has a muzzled bear carved in one of the posts.

Tyringham House, with the date 1609 carved over the staircase door, is now the village reading-room.

Before making our way north from Cuddington to all the interesting places which lie between the Thame road and Akeman Street, we can visit the handful of villages lying on the south of the River Thame, close to the Oxfordshire border. The nearest is Haddenham, a large village with a striking church overlooking the green at Church End, which has a Norman font carved with grotesque monsters, remains of fifteenth-century brasses and stained glass, much rich woodwork re-used, and two seventeenth-century mural monuments. An early seventeenth-century house in an angle of the churchyard may have been the church house.

Aston Sandford, quite close to Church End, is hardly more than a hamlet. The small church was extensively rebuilt and restored in 1877. There is a picture in the vestry of the old church of Thomas Scott, the great commentator, and grandfather of Sir Gilbert Scott, the architect, who was rector from 1801 until his death in 1838. He is buried in the church, and commemorated with a mural. Cardinal Newman wrote in his *Apologia pro Vita Sua* that Scott was the writer who 'made a deeper impression on my mind than any other, to whom (humanly speaking) I owe almost my soul'. Scott also figures in his grandson's *Recollections*. His biblical *Commentary*, commenced in 1788, was described by Sir James Stephen as 'the greatest theological performance of our age and country'.

Kingsey, on the south-west of Aston Sandford, was transferred to Oxfordshire in 1894, and transferred back to Buckinghamshire just before the outbreak of the 1939–45 war, when Towersey, a little farther to the south-west, was handed over to Oxfordshire—with the result that numerous maps and books of reference do not show them correctly. Neither has any great interest for visitors.

Ilmer, a small and compact village, has a church dating in part from the twelfth century, which has a picturesque bell-cote of weather-boarding surmounted by a shingle spire, reminiscent of Surrey churches. There are fifteenth-century sculptures on the inner jambs of the north-west window, and an attractive wooden screen, only 4 feet high, on a stone base, dating from 1500.

ii

There are several ways of exploring the countryside which lies between the Thame road and Akeman Street, and it is quite possible for those who have either plenty of time for walking, or a car, to make a 'round trip', taking in all its interesting villages.

Beginning at Cuddington, it is only a short distance to Chearsley, which is thought to be the 'Cerdic's-ley' at which Cerdic and Cynric fought with the Britons in A.D. 527. Although so old, it has never been more than a small village, with brick houses and thatched cottages climbing a steep slope. Its unspoiled little church is very simple, but attractive, with much Perpendicular work, a fine early thirteenth-century font, old timber roofs, and fifteenth-century brasses.

The church formed part of the original endowment of the abbey of Nutley or Notley, founded in the early twelfth century for Austin Canons, by Walter Giffard, which survived until the Dissolution. The ruined walls of the old abbey are built into a modern mansion on the low-flying fields beside the River Thame.

South-west of Chearsley is Long Crendon, where there was a park for beasts of the chase in 1086. There is a tradition that a castle once stood near Cop Hill. The fourteenth-century courthouse, or Staple Hall, two old manor-houses and the large church, testify to its ancient importance. This beautiful and interesting village is a stronghold of ancient custom and tradition, as more than one distinguished writer has testified. Surnames which appear in the sixteenth-century church books are still common, there is a distinctive character even in the physique of the older villagers, and such dialect as lingers suggests that there was a special racial type in this hill village. There are innumerable old houses in the village, some of which have been restored by moneyed new-comers with artistic taste. The unusually fine inn and trade signs are worth noting.

The old court house, which is close to the church, was probably first used as a wool store. Manorial Courts were held there for five or six centuries on behalf of Queen Catherine (consort of Henry V), and other lords of the manor. It is now owned by the National Trust, and the upper room, with its fine beams, is used as a Child Welfare Centre. Also near the church is a seventeenth-century manor-house, and on the south-west of the village is Long Crendon manor-house, dating in part from the early fifteenth century. There is also an interesting medieval house at Lower End.

The imposing cruciform church was almost rebuilt in the thirteenth century. There is a great sixteenth-century east window, some seventeenth-century woodwork, and a magnificent and interesting early seventeenth-century tomb with alabaster effigies of Sir John Dormer and his wife. The Dormers of Dorton became lords of the manor in 1552.

There is a direct road from Long Crendon to Shabbington, beside the Thame on the Oxfordshire border. The church is Decorated, and chiefly interesting for the herringbone masonry on the exterior of the north wall, dating from about 1100. Re-set in the modern north porch is an early fourteenth-century coffin-lid, with a worn inscription in Norman-French, but otherwise the church has no memorials.

Ickford, on the north-west, is a remote but picturesque little village full of thatched cottages, which certainly does not now deserve the slur in the old rhyme:

'Brill on the hill, Oakley in the hole,
Dirty little Ickford, shabby Worminghall.'

Ivinghoe Beacon

The Postmill, Brill

Princes Risborough

The church has a medieval saddleback tower, and has been beautifully restored. It retains its Elizabethan pulpit and tester, and has an interesting monument to Thomas Tipping, who died in 1601, and his wife and nine children, with all their figures shown in relief.

Calybute Downing, who later became a prominent Puritan Divine, was rector from 1632 to 1636, when he exchanged the living with Gilbert Sheldon, later Archbishop of Canterbury, and builder of the Sheldonian Theatre at Oxford.

William Joyner, alias Lyde, the dramatic poet, lived at Ickford between the years 1678 and 1687 in 'a most obscure, retired and devout condition'. It is said his apparel was 'little better than that of a day-labourer, and his diet and lodging were very suitable to it'. He was the great-uncle of Thomas Phillips, who was born at Ickford in 1708, and is best known as the biographer of Cardinal Pole.

South of Ickford is a seventeenth-century bridge across the River Thame. There has been a bridge on the same site since 1237.

Worminghall, the next village to be visited, also belies the old rhyme, for it is an attractive little place which seems very small and remote to have produced such celebrities as John King, Bishop of London, who was born there about 1559, and his son Henry King, Bishop of Chichester, who was born there in 1592. John was the great nephew of Robert King, first Bishop of Oxford, and is shown as one of the twelve children on the brass commemorating his father, Philip King, who died in 1592.

Henry King, the most famous of his celebrated family, was a poet and numbered Ben Jonson, Izaak Walton, and John Donne among his closest friends. His son, John King, founded some picturesque almshouses at Worminghall in 1675.

The church stands beside a large green shaded by lime and

elm-trees. It has an attractive Norman chancel arch with carved capitals, a south doorway with unusual ornament, and good Victorian imitation of medieval stained glass.

Oakley, north of Worminghall, is still in a 'hole' or valley, at the foot of Brill Hill, with meadows reaching away to the Oxfordshire border. Like its neighbours, Boarstall and Brill, it was once in the Bernwood Forest, and there are still beautiful woods in the neighbourhood. The village has a number of seventeenth-century houses, including the village school and the Sun Inn. The church was practically rebuilt in the nineteenth century. On the outside of the south wall is a fourteenth-century tomb recess with a cinquefoiled head, containing a plain slab. It is the only one of the kind in Bucks.

The numerous memorials to the Tyrrell family, who were long lords of the manor, include murals to James Tyrrell, the historical writer, who was an intimate friend of the philosopher, John Locke; and his parents Sir Timothy Tyrrell, Governor of Cardiff Castle and master of the buckhounds to Charles I, who died in 1701, and Lady Tyrrell, daughter of the famous Archbishop Usher of Armagh.

Boarstall, north-west of Oakley, has the only castle remains in all Buckinghamshire, and much else to attract us to this delightful corner of the county, with its small hills and beautiful woods.

The name of Boarstall is traditionally said to be derived from the feat of Niel or Nigel, who slew a formidable boar, and presented its head to Edward the Confessor, who granted him the custody of the Forest of Bernwood as a reward. The *Victoria County History* suggests the story is partially corroborated by the confirmation in 1266 by Henry III of a grant to the heir of the Fitz Niels said to have been held by his ancestors from the Conquest.

The manor passed to the Handlo family by marriage with the heiress of the Fitz Niels in 1299, and in 1312 licence to crenellate was given to Sir John de Handlo. An entrancing plan of Boarstall Manor, drawn about 1444 and decorated with the figures of a king and a kneeling knight with a boar's head on his sword point, is preserved for us in the *Boarstall Chartulary*.

Boarstall appears to have been rather a fortified manor than an actual castle, and was known as Boarstall House in 1644, when it gave so much trouble to the Parliamentarian army. All that now remains are the beautiful fourteenth-century gatehouse and the moat which shows the extent of the house and gardens.

The church was entirely rebuilt in 1818, but has some of the fittings of the old church, including a considerable amount of seventeenth-century woodwork and monuments to the Aubrey family. The first baronet, Sir John Aubrey, who died in 1726, and his two wives, Mary and Martha, have an inscription saying he regarded as 'the choicest blessing of Providence, and the peculiar felicity of a long life', his 'union with two women of such rare excellence'. It was the sixth baronet who rebuilt the church and pulled down Boarstall House. The manor was inherited in 1911 by Lancelot Aubrey-Fletcher, who transferred it to his son, now Sir Henry Lancelot Aubrey-Fletcher, better known as Henry Wade, the author of many distinguished and popular crime novels.

Brill, less than two miles south-west, set on a breezy hill-top nearly 700 feet above sea level, and commanding wonderful views over an enormous area of Bucks and Oxfordshire, was once a favourite hunting-box of the Saxon and Norman kings. There is a tradition that Edward the Confessor restored the sight of Wulwyn, who had made vain pilgrimages to eighty-seven churches before being healed by the saintly king. Several of the early Plantagenet kings dated Charters from Brill. Later it was granted to a succession of noble families, and in the Civil War was held for the King, until the Royalist troops were withdrawn, after which it lapsed into complete obscurity.

The palace has vanished so utterly that the site can only be guessed at; it is believed to have stood near the church; St. Werburgh's Cell has also disappeared completely; and Brill House was taken down in 1828. Nevertheless there is a manor-house dating from the fifteenth century, two seventeenth-century inns, several old houses and farms, and a seventeenth-century windmill which probably stands on the same site as the one mentioned in Domesday Book. The church was restored in 1901, but has some Norman work in the north doorway, and an Early English window, a fourteenth-century font, traces of medieval paintings, and woodwork of the fourteenth and early seventeenth centuries. There are one or two quaint inscriptions.

Brill and Ludgershall station is a mile away, and much nearer to Ludgershall, a village which once had the great John Wycliff for its rector. It is recorded at Ludgershall that he was rector from 1368 to 1390 or later, but other records say he was presented to Lutterworth, Leicestershire, in 1374.

The church has been much restored, but has remarkable fourteenth-century capitals, a Norman font, a late medieval altar tomb, and three good brasses.

The pretty little village has seventeenth-century houses and inns, and a small moated site on the south-west of the church, traditionally called King Lud's Hall. The village is said to be named after King Lud, who is also traditionally associated with the palace at Brill. A later tradition suggests that Fair Rosamond's Bower was in this district, in support of which is the name of Kingswood for an adjoining hamlet, and a lane shown on old maps as 'Rosiman's Waye'.

We can make our rather roundabout way from Ludgershall to Wotton Underwood by road or rail. Both skirt Wotton Park, which belonged to the Temple family. The house, approached by a mile-long avenue of elms, stands in a beautiful park with lakes which were probably contrived by Capability Brown. The only parts remaining of the mansion built by Richard Grenville in 1704 are the detached wings. The remainder was rebuilt in magnificent style in 1820. The fourteenth-century church which stands in the park has been practically rebuilt, but there are many monuments to the Grenville family.

We can either go direct to Ashendon from Wotton, or turn aside to visit Dorton and Chilton, and it is well worth while to see both. Dorton is a perfect little survival of a seventeenth-century community. The beautiful, many-gabled manor-house dates from 1626. It is now a school for blind children. The church is an attractive little building, with a weather-boarded bell-turret capped with a pyramidal tiled roof and some seventeenth-century panelling. The small village once had visions of a prosperous future, when a pump-room and baths were built to exploit the excellent chalybeate spring there, but the enterprise failed and the buildings were demolished.

Chilton also preserves the seventeenth-century atmosphere. It is perfectly set on a slope of the Brill Hills, and commands wide and lovely views. Chilton House was originally built in the sixteenth century, and re-faced in 1740, and is another of the possessions of the Aubrey-Fletchers. The vicarage dates from the sixteenth century, Chilton Park Farm has interesting sixteenth-century features, and the Post Office is probably of medieval origin.

The church combines good Early English, Decorated, and Perpendicular work, and is remarkable for the effigy of a knight in thirteenth-century armour, set upright on the east wall of the nave, on the outside, and visible only from the wall of the churchyard—a situation which has given rise to much speculation. There are monuments of the Croke family, who were lords of the manor from 1529 to 1682.

iii

Ashendon, which lies south-east of Wotton station, is on one of the highest hills in the Vale of Aylesbury, with its church on the summit. It is a sturdy, weather-beaten building dating from 1120. There are traces of many periods in the walls and fittings. The thirteenth-century effigy of a knight in chain mail and surcoat has not been identified with certainty. The village is small and picturesque, with a number of old thatched cottages and farmhouses. It is only about eight miles to Aylesbury from Ashendon, and by a slight deviation the return journey can be made to include visits to Lower and Upper Winchendon and Waddesdon.

Lower Winchendon, with its half-timbered, thatched, and ochre-washed cottages in the tree-shaded valley of the Thame, is an attractive picture. The sixteenth-century manor-house was altered about 1800, and re-named Winchendon Priory later in the same century. It has much of the original work, including a fine stone mantelpiece and linen-fold panelling. The fourteenth-century church is an untouched example of a village church with high pews, three-decker Jacobean pulpit, and gallery. Only the chancel has been rebuilt. It was originally a possession of Nutley Abbey, and was granted at the Dissolution to the first Earl of Bedford. It afterwards came to the Tyringhams, some of whom are buried in the church. There are some good fifteenth-century brasses. Lower Winchendon was the birthplace of Lettice, the daughter of Sir Francis Knollys, who was three times married—first to the Earl of Essex, secondly to the Earl of Leicester, whose first wife was the ill-fated Amy Robsart, and lastly to Sir Christopher Blount, who was executed in 1601. She survived until 1634, living through the reigns of seven English sovereigns.

Upper Winchendon is only a handful of cottages and a church, reached by a gated road, set on a ridge 550 feet above

sea level. Originally a possession of the Priory of St. Frides-
wide, it afterwards belonged to Wolsey, who was succeeded
by the Goodwyns, the Whartons, and the Dukes of Marlborough. The seventh Duke sold it to the Rothschild
family, who also own Waddesdon, which lies almost
opposite. The fine old manor-house was pulled down by
the third Duke of Marlborough, and even its gardens have
disappeared. The small church has a Norman door, a Perpendicular tower, and details of other periods. There is an
octagonal font, an unusual fourteenth-century pulpit, cut
from a single block of wood, and a fifteenth-century screen.
The brasses include one to Sir John Stodeley, a vicar of the
parish who died in 1502, whose effigy is shown in the habit
of an Austin Canon.

Waddesdon's old manor-house formerly stood south of
the church on Philosophy Farm, which was granted to
Oxford University towards the endowment of a lectureship
in natural philosophy, by the seventeenth-century owner of
the manor. The present manor-house was built by Baron
Ferdinand de Rothschild at the end of the nineteenth century, in the style of a French château—completely alien to
Buckinghamshire, yet curiously attractive. The influence of
the Rothschilds, like their crest of the five arrows, has pene-
trated to every corner of the village, which has been almost
completely rebuilt and is a picturesque and prosperous little
place.

The interesting church shows the development of the plan
from the twelfth century onwards, and has much fine work.
A sixteenth-century brass to Hugh Bristowe, a former
rector, has a realistic skeleton in a shroud, with a long inscription. An effigy of an armed knight has the date 1330
cut on the tomb at some later period. There is a fine brass
to Sir Roger Dynham, who died in 1490, which was
brought, with his coffin, from Eythrope in 1887. The brass
of Richard Huntyndon, another rector, who died in 1543,

portrays him in mass vestments, holding the chalice and Host. Waddesdon Park and village lie on either side of Akeman Street, along which it is only 4½ miles to Aylesbury, past Fleet Marston.

Fleet Marston has only a few farms and cottages, and a small restored church dating from the twelfth and thirteenth centuries, with a notable fifteenth-century queen-post roof in the nave. Nearby is Quarrendon, which has few inhabitants and a ruined church. As far back as 1636 it was referred to as 'an ancient enclosure depopulated', yet in past centuries the Lees of Quarrendon were a celebrated family. Sir Henry Lee built a new mansion, and entertained Queen Elizabeth with great magnificence in August 1592.

It has been suggested that Scott had Sir Henry Lee in mind when he described the Queen's Champion in *Woodstock*, Sir Henry having held a tournament annually for over thirty years, in fulfilment of his vow to uphold the honour of the Queen against all comers.

CHAPTER THIRTEEN: *Round About the Claydons*

THE deep peace and old-world beauty of the countryside which lies along the Oxfordshire border, bounded on the south by Akeman Street and on the east by the Aylesbury–Buckingham road, proclaim its neglect by the world beyond its confines.

It is a countryside of many small streams, rich pastures, ancient churches and manors, and many memories, and its neglect is all the more inexplicable when it is realized that there are no fewer than five railway stations within a radius of two miles of the Claydons!

This is a countryside which has been made dear to all lovers of memoirs by the *Memoirs of the Verney Family* by Lady Verney, which bring to life the trials and tribulations of the Civil War, the delights of the love-making of the younger generation, the thousand and one vexations attendant on household duties and servant problems, in the family which has been seated at Middle Claydon since the beginning of the sixteenth century. The last of the line died in 1810, but the name was taken by her half-sister and heiress, from whom the present-day Verneys are descended.

Sir Edmund Verney, Standard-bearer to Charles I, his sons, Sir Ralph and Sir John, and his grandson, all figure in the *Verney Memoirs*. Sir Edmund, who died at Edgehill rather than yield the standard, was said to have haunted Claydon House for many years, searching for the hand which was cut off whilst still grasping the standard. He ceased to appear when the house was so greatly altered in the eighteenth century.

The oldest part of the present house dates from the six-teenth century. One room has Carolean panelling, doorways, and chimney-piece, but the house as a whole dates from the eighteenth century, one of the most notable features being a Rococo Chinese room with a fantastic bed recess of white carved woodwork decorated with carved and coloured Chinese figures and hung with bells.

The church stands in the park, and is filled with brasses and memorials to the Verneys and earlier owners of the manor. The earliest brasses are to Isabella Giffard, who died in 1523, a priest of 1526, and Roger Giffard, who died in 1542, and is portrayed with his wife and their thirteen sons and seven daughters on one of the largest brasses in the county. It is a palimpsest on one to Walter Bellingham, a fifteenth-century Ireland King of Arms. Brasses to Sir Harry Verney, who died in 1894, and to Susan Merry, are good modern work. It was this Sir Harry, who died at the age of over ninety, active to the last, who married the sister of Florence Nightingale, and frequently entertained the famous little lady at Claydon House, discussing her reforms with deepest interest.

Among the many fine monuments in the church, the best is the lovely alabaster tomb and effigy of Margaret Giffard, who died in 1539, and a whole series of seventeenth-century monuments to the Verneys, but although Sir Edmund Verney, the Standard-bearer, is commemorated among them, his body does not lie there, as it was never recovered after Edgehill.

The Verneys acquired the other Claydons in the early eighteenth century, but had a tragic connection with East Claydon in the previous century, when Edmund Verney married Mary Abel, the heiress, and lived with her at the White House. The *Verney Memoirs* tell how she became insane, but outlived her husband and children. Their home is still a perfect example of a seventeenth-century brick house, set about with yew hedges, and moated. There are other old houses and cottages in the delightful little village, and the church has thirteenth-, fourteenth-, and fifteenth-century work.

Botolph Claydon, half a mile to the south, is a hamlet without a church, but has another old brick-and-stone manor of the Verneys, and more thatched and half-timbered cottages. *Place-names of Buckinghamshire* defines Botolph as originating in the early thirteenth century, and derives from botl, 'this particular Claydon having presumably been distinguished by some prominent "building",' and suggests that the association with St. Botolph is 'purely fictitious', although the authors admit it is impossible to say whether the Botyl Well there is derived from botl, or takes its name from St. Botolph.

Steeple Claydon, the largest of the Claydons, stands on a hill giving distant views of the Chilterns, and is dominated by its church, which is of fifteenth-century work with modern additions, including the steeple. Sir Thomas Chaloner, who was granted Steeple Claydon manor in 1557, had thrilling adventures off the coast of Barbary when only nineteen years old, which are described in Hakluyt's *Voyages*, fought at the Battle of Pinckie when twenty-six, and was knighted on the field of battle, and spent most of the rest of his life in embassies abroad. His only son was a distinguished naturalist. He went on an embassy to Scotland, where he became so great a favourite with James I that the King appointed him governor of his eldest son after he had ascended the English throne. Sir Thomas's third son, also a Thomas, was born at Steeple Claydon. During the Civil War he and his brother signed King Charles's death-warrant, and at the Restoration the manor of Steeple Claydon was granted to Sir Richard Lane, who had helped Charles II to escape after the Battle of Worcester, but another of the Chaloners bought it back in 1662.

The Manor Farm occupies the site of the manor-house of the Chaloners, and the Camp, a modern house, marks the site of the house in which Cromwell slept in 1644, before advancing to attack Hillesden House. The earthworks from which the house takes its name were probably thrown up on that occasion.

The third Thomas Chaloner, who signed the death-warrant of Charles I, founded a school at Steeple Claydon in 1656. The name of Bull Lane preserves the memory of bull-baiting days, when bulls were driven down this lane to the village. Bull-baiting took place as late as 1827 in the Chaloner school yard. The original school building was extended to form the village hall and library, towards which Florence Nightingale contributed £50. Her cheque hangs in a frame on the wall.

It is five miles from Steeple Claydon to Hillesden by road, but only a little over a mile across the fields, with the church as a landmark to guide us. Here the Verneys also play a part, for Sir Edmund married Margaret Denton, of Hillesden House. Sir Edmund Verney, of Claydon House, and his brother-in-law, Sir Alexander Denton, of Hillesden House, were practically the only great landowners in Bucks who espoused the King's cause, and, as the *Verney Memoirs* show, not all their own families fought on the King's side.

Sir Alexander Denton's wife was Mary Hampden, a cousin of John Hampden, but the manor was defended valiantly against the Parliamentarians—1,000 labourers being employed to make trenches round the house and church. When the house was captured all the inhabitants were taken prisoner and the house set on fire and burned to the ground.

Even then there were complications, with another Denton sister marrying an officer of the besieging force, Jeremiah Abercrombye, who was killed at Boarstall the following year, and buried among the cavaliers in Hillesden church. Hillesden House was rebuilt in 1648, and a later Alexander Denton, who became chancellor to the Prince of Wales (afterwards George II) in 1729, was so much beloved at Hillesden that it was said 'the best thing belonging to the place was its Master'. The mansion was pulled down by the third and last Duke of Buckingham, the then owner.

No other place in Buckinghamshire to-day is so remote as Hillesden, with a many-gated lane through grassy fields to its handful of cottages, its parsonage, and its church, but it has had an influence which has spread far and wide, for it was this beautiful Perpendicular church which inspired Sir Gilbert Scott, who was born in the neighbouring village of Gawcott, with his life-long passion for Gothic architecture. An original drawing he made of the church, when only fifteen, hangs in the vestry.

Not only the perfect proportions, but the beautiful window tracery, the remains of unusually good and complete stained glass, the fine screen, the door still showing the bullets of the Parliamentarian soldiers, and much rich carving in wood and stone, are the outstanding features contemporary with the fifteenth-century rebuilding, and there are also some elaborate monuments of various dates, including the alabaster effigies of Thomas Denton, who died in 1560, and his wife; the beautifully designed tomb of Alexander Denton, who died in 1576, and his second wife; Dr. William Denton, physician to Charles II, and a political writer, who died in 1691, at the age of eighty-six; a large and elaborate monument to Sir Alexander Denton, a justice of the Court of Common Pleas, who died in 1739, and a mural to George Woodward, 'Envoy Extraordinary from the King of Great Britain to the King and Republic of Poland', who died in Warsaw in 1735, at the age of thirty-eight. His wife Anne was a daughter of Alexander Denton.

Following another gated lane through the fields northwards, we reach Gawcott, within a mile and a half of Buckingham, where Sir Gilbert Scott's father was the first perpetual curate at the time of the architect's birth.

Sir Gilbert was born in 1811, and apart from its biographical details, his *Recollections* are well worth reading for the descriptions of life in Gawcott when he was a boy, reflecting the manners, amusements and customs of a past that has gone for ever. The church is a plain one of Classic design, built in 1828, it is said to the design of Sir Gilbert's father. Although Sir Gilbert's prodigious output included the building or restoration of thirty-eight cathedrals, abbeys and priories, 474 churches and about 200 secular buildings, including St. Pancras Station, probably his best-known work is the Albert Memorial.

The little hamlet of Lenborough has a manor-house, now a farm, which was the home of the Ingoldsby family, who were seated there from 1445, and was afterwards the property of Edward Gibbon, the historian.

Nearer the Oxfordshire border are the villages of Barton Hartshorn and Chetwode. The former is a mere hamlet, in good hunting country, with a rebuilt church, a restored seventeenth-century manor-house, and a seventeenth-century farm.

Chetwode, which also lies in the country of the Bicester Hunt, and is otherwise neglected and forgotten, has a remarkably fine church with the best Early English work in Buckinghamshire, with unusually good and complete thirteenth- and fourteenth-century stained glass, which entranced Sir Gilbert Scott in his boyhood.

Among other delightful features are the carvings of beasts and monsters on the capitals of the columns; baroque painted panels recording repairs carried out in 1820; a family pew with a fireplace; and a late eighteenth-century inscription to Risley Risley, who, among many other admirable characteristics, 'was a gentleman of great hospitality'.

The church, some fish-ponds and moats are all that remain of the Priory of Austin Canons founded in 1245, the site of which is marked by a mansion called the Priory, built in

1833. All but the church was burned in 1285 by 'certain malevolent persons', but the canons were granted protection whilst they collected alms for their relief. Five years later they were granted an annual three-day fair. In 1460 it became so poverty-stricken that it was surrendered to Nutley Abbey. The Risley family acquired the buildings, living there for many years, and apparently constantly quarrelling with the villagers, who resented their high-handed ways.

Half a mile to the north-east of the present church is the site of the old parish church it superseded, and of the hermitage of St. Stephen and St. Lawrence founded by one of the Chetwodes, who have been lords of the manor from the reign of Henry II, although not in the direct male line. Among many unusual privileges they enjoyed until modern times was the Rhyne toll, said to have originated when a Chetwode killed a huge and ferocious wild boar which had terrorized the district, then uncleared forest on the outskirts of Bernwood Forest, a feat described in an old ballad:

> Sir Rydal as he drawed his broadsword with might,
> Wind well thy horn, good hunter!·
> And he fairly cut off the boar's head quite,
> For he was a jovial hunter!

The right of the lord to claim the Rhyne toll has been upheld legally more than once, and a suit of 1577 recorded full details of the toll and its accompanying ceremonies. Horns or whelk-shells were to be blown at stated points to mark the opening of the 'Rhyne drift', when for three days all 'foreign' cattle over an area of 2,000 acres were impounded, and released only on payment of a fee. In the nineteenth century local farmers usually compounded for immunity at the rate of one shilling a year, and after the coming of the railways the proceeds were greatly diminished, and the toll was allowed to lapse soon after the opening of the twentieth century.

The traditional origin of the toll was borne out by the discovery in 1810 of the skeleton of a gigantic boar in a mound surrounded by a ditch which had long been known locally as 'boar's pond'.

The old manor-house of the Chetwodes, a picturesque building dating from 1600, and enlarged in the eighteenth century, neighbours the site of the original parish church.

A short distance east as the crow flies, but considerably farther by road, is Preston Bisset, where the Bisset family lived in the reign of Henry II. The Decorated church has some beautiful window tracery, and grotesque corbels on the chancel arch.

The village is picturesque, with thatched seventeenth-century cottages of brick and timber, or cream-wash.

Roundabout roads lead from Preston Bisset south to Twyford, worth visiting only for its church, which has a richly carved Norman doorway. There are thirteenth-century arcades, fifteenth-century woodwork, many carved corbels, and brasses and monuments, including the remnant of the effigy of a priest, the recumbent statue of a knight in chain armour, and an elaborate monument to the first Viscount Wenman, who died in 1640. The Wenmans acquired Twyford by marriage in 1550, and held it until the nineteenth century. A farmhouse stands on the site of their mansion.

The first Viscount Wenman fought gallantly at the taking of Cadiz. He was married three times, his first wife being a Roman Catholic who fell under suspicion of complicity in the Gunpowder Plot. Both she and her Protestant husband were arrested, but were able to clear themselves. She is note-worthy as the translator of a *History of the World* by John Zonaras, now in the Cambridge University Library.

South-west of Twyford is Marsh Gibbon, a large but attractive village devoted to agricultural pursuits which have left its rural character unchanged. The sixteenth-century inn

Half-timbered Inn, Bierton

Thatched Inn, Gibraltar

TYPICAL BUCKS INDUSTRIES :
Aylesbury Ducks

Wood Bodger   Pillow-lace Maker

has the original door with strap hinges; the Elizabethan manor-house has some later alterations; there is an Elizabethan tithe-barn, and Westbury Manor retains its seventeenth-century staircase and the remains of a moat nearby.

A hide of land at Marsh, or Merse, was granted by Edward the Confessor to the Abbey of Westminster, and the Norman lord bestowed the manor on the monks of Grestein in Normandy. When foreign monasteries were suppressed it came into the ownership of the De la Poles, and in 1437 they founded an almshouse at Ewelme, granting the manor as part of its endowment. It has remained in the possession of the trustees of the Ewelme almshouses.

There are fine Perpendicular windows in the south aisle of the church, and richly carved Early English capitals in the nave, but it was largely rebuilt in the nineteenth century. There is a thirteenth-century stone coffin in the north wall, and mural tablets of various periods.

We can make our way eastward from Marsh Gibbon to Edgcott, set in fields, with a fine view of the hills at Brill. There is a small, plain church, with some fragments of its old woodwork, and a corbel with a curiously carved head, but the old manor-house, dating from the late seventeenth century, and the rectory, built earlier in the same century, are more attractive. The little village is also picturesque, but a greater interest attaches to Grendon Underwood, along the road to the south, for there is an enduring tradition that Shakespeare, journeying along Akeman Street, two miles to the south, on his way to Stratford-on-Avon, turned aside to spend a night in the old Ship Inn of Grendon, now known as Shakespeare Farmhouse.

Aubrey says, 'The humour of . . . the constable in *A Midsummer Night's Dream* he happened to take at Grendon in Bucks . . . and there was living that constable about 1642 when I first came to Oxon'. Aubrey presumably meant *Much Ado about Nothing*, and Sheahan tells a circumstantial

story of the dramatist being found asleep in the church porch
by the two parish constables he afterwards immortalized as
Dogberry and Verges. It is a tradition which cannot now be
proved or disproved, but the forest track through Grendon
was certainly used by gipsies and strollers, and the mere
possibility that Shakespeare found inspiration there is enough
to set the imagination on fire.

The small church has a Perpendicular tower and an Early
English south door. There are eighteenth-century monuments to the Pigott family, including one by Scheemakers,
and one to Richard Lord Saye and Sele and his widow
Christobella.

An old couplet says: 'Grenden Underwode, The dirtiest
town that ever stode', and the members of the Bicester
Hunt would heartily agree, but in summer-time it is a
delightful place, with its fine elms and blossomy hedge-
rows.

If we make our way back to Aylesbury along Akeman
Street we shall pass the old Crooked Billet Inn with a sign-
board on which the old inscription has been repainted:

MARY HUFF

She sells good beer,

And that's enough.

A mistake here

She sells wines and spirits as well as beer.

Otherwise we can make our way by pleasant country
lanes to Quainton, an exceptionally attractive and interesting
little place backed by grassy hills, with the remains of a
fifteenth-century market cross—the only one surviving in
the county—on its village green.

The church was practically rebuilt in the nineteenth century, and interest chiefly centres on the splendid monuments
of the Winwoods, who bought Quainton Manor in 1615,
and the Dormers, who owned Shipton Manor from the

twelfth to the eighteenth century, and some mural tablets
and floor-slabs to the Pigotts, who have lived at Doddershall
House since 1503. One to Fleetwood Dormer is by Grinling Gibbons, and there is a touching one by Roubiliac
depicting Judge Dormer and his wife mourning over their
dead son—a grief which was so deep that the father died of a
broken heart the same year. Richard Winwood, who died
in 1688, is commemorated by a monument showing his
widow lying awake beside her dead husband. The monument is one of the few of that period to be signed by the
sculptor. It was by Thomas Stayner.

It was this Richard Winwood who founded the charming
almshouses which are still to be seen near the church. His
moated manor-house was partly demolished in the eighteenth century and the remainder converted into a farmhouse known as Denham Lodge.

The eighteenth-century Grange Farm marks the site of the
old home of the Dormers, which was originally the manor-
house of the Abbots of Thame.

Doddershall House, in a fine park about a mile and a half
from Quainton, dates from 1510, and is still the seat of a
descendant of Thomas Pigott who built it.

Thomas, Earl of Wharton, and his son, Philip, maintained
a race-course on Quainton Meadow in the late seventeenth
and early eighteenth centuries.

Dr. Richard Brett, the Orientalist, and one of the trans-
lators of the Authorized Version of the Bible, was Rector of
Quainton from 1595 until his death in 1637. There is a bust
to his memory in the church. George Lipscomb, the historian of Buckinghamshire, was born in the black-and-white
cottage called The Magpie in 1773. His parents are buried in
the churchyard. The historian's father was a surgeon who
had been in the Royal Navy, and had 'served in several
memorable engagements'. Lipscomb himself, after devot-
ing the best years of his life to his book, to which every later

writer on the county has been so deeply indebted, died as his history was being printed.

East of Quainton is Pitchcott, enchantingly set on a hill commanding wide views southward. Its church has been restored. Its neighbour Oving, which is a very pretty village, equally beautifully situated, has an interesting little church, which was held until the Dissolution by the Priory of St. John of Jerusalem in England. There is a Perpendicular Screen, four oak benches dating from the fifteenth century, traces of a fourteenth-century wall-painting, and carved bosses on the oak roof of the nave. A memorial tablet commemorates Henry Lovebond, 'who was distinguished for his learning and integrity and those other virtues which are the ornaments of human life'.

There is an Elizabethan manor-house near the church, and Oving House is a fine eighteenth-century mansion. The Black Boy Inn and several of the smaller houses in the village date from the late sixteenth century.

Oving has always been noted for its pasture, and in the sixteenth century the lords of the manor and some of their freeholders created a common, to be known as the cow pasture and used for their mutual benefit. There were proceedings in Chancery during the reign of Elizabeth, when Robert Carter of North Marston was accused of taking 'in some sort of outrageous behaviour . . . the grass growing upon the same ground with the mouths of his beasts'.

On the crest of the hill above the village is the meeting-place of five roads, the famous *quinque-via* of old manuscripts, and two miles to the north of Oving is North Marston, long a place of pilgrimage as the shrine of an early rector, Master John Shorne, who died in 1314. An old rhyme perpetuates his memory:

> Sir John Shorne
> Gentleman borne
> Conjured the devil into a horn

or, as some versions of his feat say, into a boot. So great was his popularity as a local saint, and so many pilgrimages were made to his shrine, that the Dean and Canons of Windsor carried it off to St. George's Chapel in 1478. His name is perpetuated in the Shorne Wells, a chalybeate spring of very pure water, which supplies North Marston well, and by the figures of the saint, the devil, and the boot, depicted on many stained-glass windows in churches in all parts of England.

It was probably due to Shorne's fame that the church developed into the beautiful example of Perpendicular work it remains to-day. There are some remarkable gargoyles on the exterior. An extremely unusual monument on the north wall of the chancel to the memory of John Virgin, a former rector who died in 1694, consists of a hand pointing downwards, with the inscription 'He lise just downe thare', and a touching little inscription dating from 1613, from a doctor, John Saunders, in memory of his wife, commences:

> This small monument,
> Though nor my skill, nor prayers, could save
> Thyself, grave matron, from the grave,
> Yet he takes care thy virtues lie
> Engraven in brass, and never die.

There are some good brasses, old books, and other interesting features, and brilliant glass in the east window, given by Queen Victoria to commemorate John Camden Neild, who had left her the whole of his fortune of over half a million pounds.

Neild had inherited North Marston and other properties from his father, James Neild, the famous prison reformer and philanthropist, and had spent the last thirty years of his life in accumulating wealth. He wore old clothes, and would never allow them to be brushed, because he said it destroyed the nap, and always went on foot to his estates. He never spent a shilling on his farms, and exacted the utmost farthing of rent, and in addition always stayed with his tenants, sharing their meals, however poor.

Grandborough, half-way between North Marston and Winslow, has some old brick cottages set in wide pastures, and a church restored by Sir Gilbert Scott, which has regained two rare treasures—a fifteenth-century alabaster panel of the Crucifixion, which had been built into the gable of a house in the village, and a leaden chrismatory, which was found during the restoration of the church built into the chancel wall. It has three receptacles, two of which retain their lids, for the three oils, 'oleum sanctum', 'oleum infirmatorium', and 'oleum chrisma', used before the Reformation in the ceremonies of baptism, confirmation, and extreme unction. It is an extremely rare and interesting relic.

All the interior walls of the church are covered with Victorian murals, and in the churchyard is a gravestone with an inscription to Mrs. Elizabeth Rutland, who died in 1723 at the age of 32, but whose age is shown as 232!

It is only two miles from Grandborough to Winslow station.

FOUR miles north of Aylesbury the road to Buckingham passes the low hill on which Hardwick is set. The village has character, and the church, with its fourteenth-century tower of white limestone and traces of very early work in the nave, possibly of pre-Conquest date, is of considerable architectural interest. There is a fine alabaster monument to Sir Robert Lee, who died in 1616, and his wife, with their effigies, and the figures of eight sons and six daughters. Many members of the Lee family in the United States are descended from this Sir Robert. In the vestry is an old chest, and the photograph of a fourteenth-century jug, now in the County Museum at Aylesbury, which was found in a secret chamber when the church was restored.

Thomas Wood, the celebrated lawyer, was rector of Hardwick from 1704 until his death in 1722. He was a nephew of Anthony à Wood, the antiquary, and was himself a prolific writer, his best-known work being his *Institute of the Laws of England*, which was for many years a leading work on English law.

A mural tablet outside the south wall of the church commemorates the re-burial there, in 1818, of the men who fell at the Battle of Aylesbury in 1643, by Lord Nugent, who lived for thirty-five years in the neighbouring hamlet of Weedon, in a mansion known as 'Lilies'. In addition to his *Biography of Hampden*, Lord Nugent wrote *Legends of the Library of Lilies*. There is a tradition that two monasteries known as 'Lilies' and 'Roses' stood there in the Middle Ages, but there appears to be no documentary record of these buildings.

Another mile along the main road brings us to Whitchurch, a long village on a low ridge above the road, dominated by its church. There are a number of interesting old houses. One, dating from the time of Queen Anne, has stone mermaids over the front door. Another, known as the Sycamores, was the home of Dr. Lipscomb, author of the *History of Buckinghamshire*, who was in practice there.

The mound on which the old castle of Bolebec stood, together with earthworks and the sites of the drawbridges, can still be traced on the south side of Market Hill, partly in the grounds of the Grange. At the outer edges of the moat is a spring called 'Fair Alice'. In virtue of the importance of the castle, Whitchurch was a market town and borough in very early days, but little of its history is known, its prosperity having declined when the feudal lord ceased to live there.

The church dates from the early thirteenth century, with some of its early furnishings, brasses, and monuments surviving. There is a painting of St. Margaret, and a tablet to John Westcar, who died in 1833, with the well-carved figures of a man with an ox and three sheep, and the inscription:

> 'Unblemished let me live, or die unknown:
> Oh, grant an honest fame, or grant me none.'

Westcar was celebrated in his day for the prize cattle he raised on the Creslow Pastures, the most famous grazing land in Bucks from time immemorial. One of his prize oxen exhibited at Smithfield Show in 1799 was sold for £100—a huge sum in those days.

The enormous Creslow pastures stretch north-eastward from the hill on which Whitchurch is set. One field alone is 300 acres in extent, and from the time of the Tudors to the Commonwealth the sheep and oxen for the use of the royal household were pastured there. The keeper of the royal pastures usually lived in the manor-house, which is still used

as a farm. It is probably the oldest surviving domestic building in the county, and one of the oldest in England. The
greater part dates from the early fourteenth century, although remodelled and enlarged in the seventeenth century,
probably by Cornelius Holland, the regicide.

On the north-west of the manor-house is the nave of the
old parish church, dating back to the twelfth century, when
it belonged to the priory of St. John of Jerusalem, who
retained it until the Dissolution. By the reign of Elizabeth
the congregation had declined, the rectory was suppressed,
and services were no longer celebrated. In 1786 it was used
as a dovecot, and shortly afterwards was adapted as a coach-
house.

Hoggeston, a mile or two beyond Whitchurch, is a small,
compact village with brick and timber-framed cottages, an
early seventeenth-century manor-house with plaster-decor-
ated pediments and some delightful farmhouses. The church
and eighteenth-century rectory stand inside an old earthwork. The church has been rather too thoroughly restored,
but there are Norman piers and some Decorated windows,
and an effigy which may be that of one of the de Birmingham
family who came into possession of the manor in the
thirteenth century. The effigy is shown holding a model of a
church in his hands, which is believed to indicate he is
Sir William de Birmingham, who founded a chantry in the
church, and died in 1342.

Among other interesting features are the octagonal fifteenth-century font, the pulpit, dating from 1700, a brass
dated 1608, and an elaborate altar tomb, three seventeenth-
century panels converted into an umbrella stand and an old
'tussock', resembling a hassock in shape and size, but formed
of a thick slab of dried, peaty soil covered with rushy grass,
a survival from those used some three or four centuries ago.

It is possible either to follow the main road direct to
Winslow, or make a pleasant detour through Swanbourne.

None of its black-and-white cottages is earlier than the seventeenth century, for in the Civil War 'a number of armed men calling themselves the King's Forces, under the command of the Earls of Cleveland and Carnarvon . . . burnt the village of Swanbourne and murdered a poor woman there and, seeming to take delight in the desolation they caused, set guards to prevent anyone from attempting to quench the flames'.

However, the Manor-House, the Old House, and a number of farms in the near neighbourhood are of sixteenth-century work, and the church is Early English with later additions. There are two early seventeenth-century brasses, one of which has an inscription to Thomas Adams:

'Who in prime of youth by bloudy theves was slain,
 In Liscombe ground his bloud ye grass did staine.'

There is an exceptional number of interesting epitaphs in the church. The modern wall-tablets to members of the Fremantle family include one to the memory of Admiral Sir Thomas Fremantle, a Buckinghamshire man who was one of Nelson's admirals. He was severely wounded at Santa Cruz in the same engagement as that in which Nelson lost his arm, both admirals being nursed by Mrs. Fremantle on the voyage home. Their eldest son was created a baronet in 1821 in acknowledgment of his father's services, and fifty-three years later was created Lord Cottesloe. It was he who first owned the manor of Swanbourne. The third Lord Cottesloe was one of the original members of the Bucks County Council, and was the only Bucks County Councillor still a member at the celebration of its Jubilee in 1939.

Winslow is so quiet and unassuming that in spite of its many old houses and its charming air of settled peace, it is hard to realize it has been in existence for at least 1200 years. By the end of the eighth century there was a palace of the Mercian Kings there. It was whilst staying there in 792 that Offa drew up his plans for founding the monastery of St. Albans and granted it his royal estate of Wuineshauue. The abbey held Winslow until the Dissolution, and in 1234 gained a market and fair for the town, both of which have continued to the present day. The oldest inn is the Bell Hotel, first mentioned about the beginning of the seventeenth century. Both the Market House and the George Hotel, dating from the eighteenth century, have iron balconies of elaborate scrollwork, said to have been brought from Claydon House.

Winslow Hall was built by William Lowndes—whose name, and the date 1700, are on the frieze over the door— from the designs of either Inigo Jones or Sir Christopher Wren. Lowndes, whose family had been settled at Winslow since the sixteenth century, was born there in 1652, and was educated in Buckingham. He began his lifelong connexion with the Treasury about 1679, and is best remembered as 'Ways and Means' Lowndes, from a phrase he is said to have originated, which is incorporated in the family arms. There are a number of tombs to the Lowndes family in the church. The church dtaes from about 1320, and contains some good brasses, the remains of fifteenth-century wall paintings, and a small but good library, including a black-letter commentary dated 1508.

Interesting as the church is, the old Baptist Chapel, dating from 1695, is even more worthy of note, for it retains all its original wooden fittings arranged on the old Calvinistic plan.

Between Winslow and Buckingham by-ways lead to Addington and Adstock. Addington has a restored church with some interesting monuments, and fifty panels of early seventeenth-century Flemish glass set in borders of pink grisaille glass during the Victorian restoration of the church. The Victorian mansion, in a beautiful upland park, incorporates panelling from the earlier manor-house on the site.

The fine cruciform tithe-barn near the house is the only one in the county.

Robert Whitehall, the poetaster, whose father was rector of Addington from 1616 to his death, lived at the rectory there for some time, and Luke Heslop, rector of Adstock, was also rector of Addington.

Adstock still has some picturesque thatched cottages near the church, of which the older part dates from the twelfth century. The octagonal Perpendicular font has a rose on each panel, and the remains of the ancient rood-screen have been inserted in the panels of the pulpit. Mural monuments commemorate three Thomas Egertons who, between them, held the living for 120 years between 1569 and 1720, and Alexander Burrell, who was rector for fifty years until his death in 1771.

Luke Heslop, who wrote on enclosures and their effect in 1801, was rector from 1778 to 1803, and Charles Neate, the economist and political writer, was born there in 1806. Witty, kind, and chivalrous, he invariably championed the cause of the weaker side. At one time a well-known rider and steeplechaser, he was also a gifted scholar, writing French with an elegance admired by the French themselves. It was at Adstock he acquired his life-long love of field sports.

Back on the main road, we pass the Folly Inn, near which a detachment of Parliamentary troops, under Colonel Middleton, was defeated by a regiment of horse commanded by Sir Charles Lucas.

Padbury, on a low hill, stretches for over half a mile between the main road and the station, which lies on the west, close to the Claydon Brook. The roads from Winslow, Steeple Claydon, Thornborough, and Buckingham meet at Padbury, and although there is no evidence of its having been a market town, it has an air of distinction. There are houses of all periods from the sixteenth century onwards, from thatched and half-timbered brick cottages to charming colour-washed and thatched Victorian estate cottages. The manor-house, now a farm, probably occupies the site of the original manor-house mentioned in 1248, and the early seventeenth-century Corn Mill the site of a mill recorded in 1086. The church is also a blending of all periods from 1210 onwards, and has fascinating carved corbels and traces of fourteenth-century paintings.

The Priors of Bradwell were patrons of the church in the thirteenth century, and there were constant disputes between the Priors and the vicars. On one occasion, when the parsonage of Padbury had been 'wrongfully let, rent free' to Thomas Darell by John Wells (Prior of Bradwell from 1492 to 1503), a forcible entry was made to turn the vicar out.

The countryside creeps very close to the little town of Buckingham, and the green meadows and trees enhance the mellow warmth of the old brick houses, with their attractive tiled roofs. It is a captivating little place in which to linger, and as a touring centre is in complete harmony with the old-world villages of the countryside around. The remote and secluded site, which proved so fatal to its aspirations as a county town, has made it ideal as a survival of a more leisurely and beauty-loving age.

There is no doubt of its antiquity, yet little is known of its history before the Conquest, when it sprang into Domesday Book as a fully-fledged county town. It was probably already in existence when Edward the Elder formed his shires, fortifying Buckingham as the shire town, and giving its name to the hundreds allotted to it.

There are legends associating Buckingham with St. Rumbold in the seventh century, but the name of the town first occurs in recorded history in the *Anglo-Saxon Chronicle*, which records that in 918, '. . . before Martinmas, went King Edward to Buckingham with his army, and sat there four weeks, during which he built the two forts on either side of the water, ere he departed thence'.

Ethelred II, who became king in 978, established a mint there, some of the coins from which can be seen in the museum at Aylesbury, and coins were also minted there in the time of Cnut.

Nevertheless, the inconvenience of having the county town at the extreme north of the county was soon realized, and much of the county work was done at Aylesbury. This, together with the fact that the Norman lords of the castle were never in residence, led to the decline of Buckingham's importance in county affairs, although it developed a flourishing wool and cloth trade. Flemish weavers obtained licence to live in the town in 1436, and a Drapers' Hall was established in the market-place.

By 1540 there had been a decline in prosperity, but ten years later the borough obtained a charter of incorporation and entered on a new era of prosperity. When Queen Elizabeth paid the town a visit in August 1578 she was welcomed with great ceremony, and proceeded 'in most triumphant manner her sword royal and maces born and trumpets blown before her till she came to the mansion house of the rectory or parsonage of the same borough, where her highness rested dinner-time'.

Curiously enough, although the Corporation were royalists, and there was great coming and going of the troops of both sides, Buckingham suffered comparatively little during the Civil War. Charles I stayed there with his army for four days in 1644. Cromwell passed several weeks in the town after the siege of Hillesden House, but the chief local excitement of the war was the plundering of Sir Richard Minsull's house at Bourton by the Parliamentarians, whilst he was away from home.

After the Restoration, Buckingham blossomed out as a social centre. The wealthy landowners of the surrounding countryside made it their centre, and the Assembly Rooms were graced with a glittering company, even his Grace of

Buckingham condescending to come over from Stowe. A stage-coach service was instituted between Buckingham and London which did the return journey in four days.

Pepys rode to Buckingham with W. Hewer on 8 June 1668, and thought it 'a good old town', but has little else to say about it, and it is to Thomas Baskerville we must go for a good contemporary account. He described it as a pretty large town with good inns, surrounding a green mound with some ruins of the castle.

In March 1725 Buckingham had its worst set-back, when a fire destroyed 138 out of the 387 houses in the town, but later in the century Buckingham had two of its most zealous friends, Lord Cobham, who succeeded in getting the summer assizes transferred there, and Browne Willis, who was Member of Parliament for the borough from 1705 to 1708, the casting vote for his election being made by a man brought from prison for the purpose. The antiquary never ceased his labours for the town which had done him this honour, and secured it many benefits. He also wrote the *History and Antiquities of the Town, Hundred, and Deanery of Buckingham*, which is a mine of information. His funeral in 1760 was attended in state by the corporation.

Buckingham was fortunate in preserving its character all through the nineteenth century, although the tan-yard, wool-yard, and lace-industry which flourished there at the beginning of the century gradually declined, and development was made on new lines with the opening up of trading facilities. The coming of a branch of the Grand Junction Canal in 1801 was celebrated by a large party given by the Marquess of Buckingham at the Cobham Arms Inn . . . and a liberal supply of beer was given to the populace'. The opening of the railway in 1850 gave the town a further impetus, and it has settled down to a quiet prosperity as a market town for a great agricultural district.

It is hard to understand Lipscomb's strictures on Buckingham, for it must have looked much the same in his day, and its charm is very apparent to our eyes, with the River Ouse almost encircling it, and the wealth of trees and flowers in its old walled gardens adding to the charm of spacious streets and market square. Although the greater part of the town dates from the rebuilding after the fire in the eighteenth century, there are some interesting survivals of an earlier date.

The Chapel of St. John the Baptist, at one time used as a Latin School, dates from the end of the twelfth century, with alterations made in the fifteenth century. It is now in the care of the National Trust. The Town Hall, built in the late seventeenth century by Sir Ralph Verney, M.P. for the town, has a clock-tower surmounted by a gigantic gilded swan, with its wings outstretched, the crest of the county. The old borough gaol was built by Lord Cobham, at his own expense, in 1748, to support Buckingham's claim to have the summer assizes held there. It is now the fire-station.

The surviving sixteenth-century houses are chiefly to be found in Church Street, climbing up to the church which marks the site of the old castle. Unfortunately it is a not very good example of late eighteenth-century work, and is the least interesting of the older buildings in the town. It stands imposingly on its hill, but has no monuments, and only the most fragmentary pieces of woodwork from the old church. Its most notable feature is the east window, set up by the Buckingham Needle and Thread Society, which also gave the reredos and other decorative work, but its real treasure is the beautiful manuscript bible with the illuminated inscription, 'Given to the Chancel of Buckingham Church by John Rudyng in 1471'. Originally chained to a desk in the church, it was subsequently stolen. Long afterwards it came into the hands of Browne Willis, and after his death was bought back by the then vicar.

The oldest inns are the White Hart, the Three Cups, and

the Fleece, but they have been much altered. Most of the other buildings in the town are of eighteenth-century architecture at its most attractive, particularly the cottages which mark the site of the old Bull Ring and are still known by that name.

The Castle House, in West Street, although refronted in the reign of Queen Anne, dates back to the fifteenth or late fourteenth century, and has associations with Catherine of Aragon, who stayed there in 1514, and Charles I. Cromwell is reputed to have stayed at the Corner House, opposite, during his visit. The manor-house dates from the same period, and has a queer, twisted chimney dating from 1520, the like of which can only be seen at Hampton Court. The old vicarage, dating from the time of Charles II, has a wonderfully carved black marble mantelpiece.

Apart from its close association with the Earls and Dukes of Buckingham, whose great mansion of Stowe is linked to the town by its famous avenue of elms and beeches, Buckingham had several 'worthies' of local fame, of whom the most picturesque was 'the Learned Taylor of Buckingham', Robert Hill, who bought a Latin Grammar with the first money he earned, and ran errands for the boys of the Latin School in exchange for help in his studies. He later learned Greek and Hebrew. On his death in 1777, at the age of seventy-eight, it was said 'though buried in obscurity and scarce subsisting by his labour, he was perfectly contented, extremely modest and diffident in his discourse'.

CHAPTER FIFTEEN: *Roads from Buckingham*

BUCKINGHAM is the meeting-place of five main roads, and an excellent centre for exploring the north of the county.

Tingewick stretches along both sides of the Bicester road. Its church, in spite of some Norman work, has no great interest, except to the lover of brasses, who will find a notably good early seventeenth-century example to Erasmus Williams, a former rector. It is full of minute detail, with designs symbolical of his attainments in music, painting, astronomy, and geometry, and a long, eulogistic epitaph.

North of Tingewick is the hamlet of Water Stratford, in the Upper Ouse Valley, with picturesque cottages, a manor-house dating in part from 1598, a seventeenth-century farm, and a small church which, although rebuilt in 1828, has attractive Perpendicular windows and two Norman doorways re-set in the new fabric. The wonderfully vigorous designs of the tympana are of late twelfth-century work.

There is an early seventeenth-century monument on the north wall of the nave to a woman who died in child-bed, depicting her in bed, with her family standing round her. Among those buried in the church is John Mason, who was rector from 1674 to his death in 1694. In his younger days he was a Calvinist with wide sympathies, and a distinguished hymn-writer, but after the death of his wife he became a fanatic, preaching a Second Advent at Water Stratford. Many people fell under the spell of his preaching, left their homes, sold their property, and went to live at Water Stratford in barns and tents on a plot of ground called the 'Holy Ground', to await the day of judgment. Noisy meetings were held, and dancing and singing were kept up day and night at the parsonage. His followers were so firmly convinced of the truth of his prophecy that he would rise from the dead after three days that they refused to believe in his death. Even when his successor had the grave opened and the body exposed, many remained unconvinced. The 'Holy Ground' was finally cleared by force, but meetings were held in the village for at least sixteen years afterwards. Joseph Bosworth, Rawlinson Professor of Anglo-Saxon at Oxford, was rector from 1857 until his death, and is buried in the churchyard.

The Roman road from Bicester to Towcester passed through the parish, and a number of Roman remains were found when digging for the railway viaduct. In a field behind Water Stratford House are trenches which may have been part of a prehistoric camp.

The only other village on the banks of the Ouse in its winding course to Buckingham is Radclive, an attractive little place with a handsome seventeenth-century manor-house, now a farm, an ancient manorial mill on the riverside, and a church with a good fourteenth-century tower, and much old material re-set at the restoration in 1903. The font is Norman, and there is a very fine Queen Anne mahogany chest bound with brass. The remains of the fourteenth-century glass include figures of the Virgin and Child, and a rose with red and green petals. The altar table is fronted with an elaborately carved panel from a seventeenth-century chest.

ii

Foscott, the first village reached by way of the Towcester road, lies down a lane, north of the road, and on the very edge of the valley of the Ouse. The church is small and ancient, but has been much restored, and only the south doorway remains from the original Norman church. There are fourteenth-century corbels and fragments of sixteenth-century glass. An early fourteenth-century bell hangs at the west end of the nave.

Leckhampstead, also north of the main road, is close to the Northamptonshire boundary, down a secluded country lane. The scattered village lies in a little valley, and a mill-stream flows by the attractive church with its richly carved Norman doorway and other interesting details. The Norman tympanum is carved with two dragons fighting over a long-eared human figure; an octagonal Norman font has carving added two centuries later, and there are traces of thirteenth-century paintings. Two brasses have effigies of the early sixteenth century, one of which has only been restored to the church in recent years, and there is a table tomb with the effigy of a knight in armour dating from the early fourteenth century. A medieval sanctus bell hangs in the north aisle.

Thornton, south of the main road, is also right on the county boundary, beside the River Ouse, which widens to a small lake in front of Thornton House. Built about 1850, and incorporating part of an older building, Thornton House is set in a fine park, with the church in its grounds, approached by an avenue of pines. Neither the house nor the church, which was largely rebuilt at the same time, are typical of Bucks, but have the charm of peace and seclusion. The church has brasses and monuments from the earlier building. Robert Ingylton, who died in 1472, is shown with his three wives, and there is an effigy of a woman in the costume of about 1557. The mid-fifteenth-century alabaster effigies of John Barton and his wife show him in plate armour, and her in a sleeveless dress and long cloak. Some of the brasses and effigies described by Browne Willis have since disappeared.

A road from Thornton running north near the county boundary, here marked by the leisurely windings of the River Ouse, passes Beachampton and Calverton on its way to Stony Stratford, or a return to Buckingham can be made by way of Thornborough.

Beachampton's church, though so remote, has not escaped

restoration. It was practically rebuilt in 1873. The timber bell-chamber and shingled spire are still delightfully picturesque. There is a quaint brass to 'William Bawdyn, Blacksmyth', who died in 1600. Alice Baldwyn, who died in 1611, is shown with her four children; and William Elmer, who founded a school in the parish and a charity for clothing sixteen poor men and women, has a brass dated 1652. An elaborate monument showing a figure in grave-clothes commemorates Matthew Pigott, a former rector, who died in 1598; and a white marble bust on a black marble pedestal under a Classical canopy commemorates Sir Simon Benet, who died in 1631, but the monument was not put up until 1759. He had been a great benefactor to University College, Oxford, who belatedly acknowledged their indebtedness with this bust, which shows him in a large wig and long lace cravat of more than a century after his death.

Hall Farm, which lies north of the church, dates principally from the early seventeenth century, but marks the site of an earlier manor-house. It has a splendid contemporary staircase, an oak-panelled banqueting hall, some large open fireplaces, and old stained glass. The whole village, though small, is full of charming corners, with its thatched cottages, trees, and small streams.

Calverton, now practically a suburb of modern Stony Stratford, is a pleasant little place with a stately manor-house, now a farm, built in 1500 and enlarged by later owners. The church was completely rebuilt between 1818 and 1824, and is a sumptuous example of the mid-Victorian style, with elaborate wood and stone carving, brilliant polychrome colouring on the interior walls, and much good Victorian stained glass, mosaics, and other decorative colouring. Strangely enough, both manor and church have associations with murders, although the latter is more remote.

The widow of Simon Bennett, a Roundhead who had received a pardon at the Restoration, and died in 1682, inherited 'a most prodigious estate'. She continued his policy of enclosing the common fields and converting them to pasture, and it was said in a lawsuit of 1692 that she kept a large amount of plough lands 'in her owne hands laid downe and untilled so that the parish is almost depopulated and the fields looke like a wildernesse'. It did her little good, however. Whilst living by herself in Calverton manor-house, 'a miserable, covetous, and wretched person . . . being supposed to have great Store of Money by her, tempted a Butcher of Stony Stratford to get artfully into the House, and as there was no Body to assist her or call for Help he barbarously murthered her on 19 September 1694'.

The Hon. Charles George Perceval, who was rector of the parish from 1820 to 1858, built the south aisle of the church and the neighbouring almshouses. He was a grandson of the Earl of Egmont, and nephew of Spencer Churchill, the Prime Minister who was murdered in the lobby of the House of Commons. The death of the Prime Minister and other direct heirs brought the rector into the line of succession, and his son eventually became the seventh Earl. The rectory was built in 1820 on the site of a Roman camp.

iii

Thornborough is an enchanting village of thatched, yellow-washed cottages and inns grouped round its green, complete with stocks, and a little stream wandering from side to side of the main streets. The New Inn, Manor Farm, and manor-house are all interesting examples of seventeenth-century building. The church has traces of Norman work, but was largely rebuilt between the thirteenth and fifteenth centuries. There is a fourteenth-century brass, fragments of fifteenth-century stained glass, and a converted Georgian barrel organ.

A mile away on the Buckingham Road is the only medieval bridge of importance in Bucks—a handsome six-arched bridge built in the fourteenth century, across a tributary of the Ouse. It is only 12 feet wide, and modern traffic has to cross in single file.

Nearby are the Thornborough Mounds, in which Roman remains were found in 1839.

iv

The main avenue of Stowe House, nearly two miles long, is on the north-west of Buckingham, and is entered through a Corinthian arch 60 feet wide.

The enormous mass of Stowe House and its 500 acres of grounds was developed over more than half a century, but always in the same style, and it now stands as one of the most complete and perfect expressions of eighteenth-century taste in the grand manner. Robert Adam, Vanbrugh, Gibbs, Leoni, William Kent, and others of the greatest architects of the eighteenth century played their part in the design of the house and its many ornamental pavilions, whilst 'Capability Brown', who had been a gardener there, transformed the grounds into the landscapes which delighted eighteenth-century taste. Pope and other poets of the day praised their beauties, and Thomson refers to them in the *Seasons* as 'wide extended'.

Stowe came into the possession of the Temple family about 1590. The grandson of the first owner was one of the first four to be created a baronet. The second baronet took the side of Parliament in the early days of the Civil War, but resigned his commission on the execution of the King. It was during the time of his son, Sir Richard, that Celia Fiennes visited the house, and left an account of its appearance in 1694. His son and heir, another Richard, was created Lord Cobham for his services in the Flemish wars, and began the development of Stowe House.

Lord Cobham was succeeded by his sister, Hester, Viscountess Cobham and Countess Temple, whose son and heir was the friend and brother-in-law of Pitt, the great Earl of Chatham. Lord Temple, on his retirement from public life, amused himself with the improvement of his house and garden at Stowe, 'a sort of mania with the family', and was responsible for the magnificent south front as it stands to-day—nearly 1000 feet long and in perfect proportion, with splendid interior decorations to match its impressive façade.

He, too, entertained largely, and commemorated his visitors with statuary, monumental arches, and inscriptions, for which he had a passion at which Horace Walpole was never tired of poking fun.

In 1784 the Temples of Stowe became Marquesses of Buckingham, and in 1822 were created Dukes of Buckingham and Chandos, but the second duke through unfortunate speculations lost the greater part of his fortune. The third and last duke died in 1889, and Stowe was then leased to the exiled Comte de Paris, grandson of Louis Philippe, and heir apparent to the French throne, who died there in 1894.

Stowe House was opened as a public school for boys in 1923. It is a pleasant gesture that the trees of the great avenue were saved from destruction through their purchase by Eton College, which presented them to the school. The new chapel, added in 1927, is a striking example of a modern development of the Classical style, by Sir Robert Lorimer. The old church, which also stands in the park, has brasses and monuments to the Temple family, but, with the exception of one dating from 1619, they are not on the elaborate scale the splendours of the house would suggest. Stowe Castle, east of the park, is an early nineteenth-century 'folly'.

Shalstone, four and a half miles from Buckingham, lies just north of the main road. It is a pretty little village of stone cottages and much thatch, a late Georgian manor-house, and old farms. The church was entirely rebuilt in the nineteenth century, chiefly by Sir Gilbert Scott, but has numerous monuments. There is a bust of Elizabeth Purefoy by

Richard Batchelor, of Buckingham, a tablet by Nollekens, and two by Westmacott, and a brass effigy dated 1540, commemorating Dame Susan Kynestone, which is the only brass in Bucks to a 'vowess'. The registers were described by Browne Willis as the most remarkable he had seen.

The Purefoys acquired Shalstone in 1418, and remained until Henry Purefoy, the last of the direct line, and 'a Gentleman possessed of many excellent qualities, and fond of retirement', who 'conversed more with Books than men', died in 1762. The manor passed in the female descent successively to the Jervoise and the FitzGerald families. The *Purefoy Letters*, written over a period from 1725 to 1753, and published in 1931, have invested the manor with all the charm of a home of old and loved friends.

Set above the winding Ouse, which here defines the boundary between Buckinghamshire, Oxfordshire, and Northamptonshire, Westbury is a pretty little village with a rebuilt manor-house, and a restored church. Charles I marched through Westbury with an army of 4,000 foot, 4,000 horse, and ten guns, on his way to the Battle of Copredy Bridge. There is a tradition that Sir Thomas Lyttelton, the then owner, suffered for his loyalty to the Royalist cause, and his son was compelled to sell the manor to the Price family, one of whom built the bridge over the Ouse. It is an earlier owner, however, whose name carries with it a breath of romance, for in 1613 it was bought by Laurence Washington, the second son of Laurence Washington of Sulgrave Manor, from whom George Washington was descended. It is true the Washingtons sold it again in 1639, but Laurence's son, Justinian, was baptised at Shalstone in 1624, which seems to show the family was actually living there at the time

Following the Ouse, which flows in a wide bend along the county boundary, we come to Turweston, on the northwest, right on the Northamptonshire boundary. It is a pretty little place, with a tree-shaded green, an interesting church, and an early seventeenth-century manor-house. The church has Norman, Early English, and Decorated work, with rich Victorian fittings of the 1863 period, and brasses of a priest in mass vestments of the early fifteenth century, and Thomas Grene and his wife, dated 1470. A marble monument to Simon Haynes, who died in 1628, depicts him and his wife kneeling at the prie dieu, with a child on a low bed in front.

Still skirting the border of the county along the valley of the Ouse, we reach Biddlesden, where a well-proportioned eighteenth-century mansion marks the site of the manor-house built from the materials of the Cistercian abbey founded in 1147 by Ernald de Roscoe. The church, which was originally used as a private chapel, also dates from the eighteenth century, and both stand in a well-wooded park.

From Biddlesden we can make our way to Lillingstone Dayrell and Lillingstone Lovell, two quiet hamlets in beautifully wooded country, which take their names from the families who were their respective lords of the manor—the Dayrells from the twelfth century until 1885, and the Lovells during the fourteenth century only.

Lillingstone Dayrell has by far the most interesting church, with many memorials to the Dayrells. The earliest dates from 1491, with inscribed brasses. A fine sixteenth-century table tomb has the effigies of Paul Dayrell and his wife, with shields of arms and the kneeling figures of their nine sons and six daughters, and is decorated with carved elephants' heads.

The Old Tile House, built by Sir Marmaduke Dayrell between 1693 and 1697, is a fine example of the brickwork of that period. At Chapel Green, two miles away, are the remains of the fifteenth-century chapel of St. Thomas of Canterbury, which belonged to the now vanished Benedictine Luffield Priory, which stood nearby.

Lillingstone Lovell formed a detached part of Oxfordshire until 1844, and still belongs to the hundred of Ploughley. The attractive little Decorated church is one of the only three in Bucks with a saddle-back roof on the tower.

There is a Jacobean pulpit, box pews, hatchments, and good brasses. The earliest has two hands rising from clouds, holding a bleeding heart, to the memory of John Merstun, a former rector, who died in 1446; effigies of Thomas Clarell with his wife and three children, date from the end of the fifteenth century, and show him with a collar of suns and roses, the only example of this order in Buckinghamshire; and one of his sons in vestments. The Rev. William Lloyd, who was rector for sixty-three years, presented the ancient pewter sacramental vessels to the Buckinghamshire Archæological Society.

The village lies beside a little stream, on fields sloping down to Wicken Wood on the Northamptonshire border, within half a mile of the main road back to Buckingham, which runs south through the pleasant village of Akeley, with its rebuilt church, to Maids Moreton, which derives its name from a tradition that the church was entirely rebuilt in 1450 through the munificence of two maiden ladies, daughters of the last Thomas Pever. A house near the Manor Farm is traditionally their home, in spite of the fact that it appears to have no work earlier than the sixteenth century.

Maids Moreton is only a mile and a half from Buckingham station, and has naturally developed as a residential suburb, but it has contrived to keep its rural atmosphere.

The church is one of the few in the county dating entirely from one century, and has great dignity and harmony of design. The west tower, which Sir Gilbert Scott praised as 'of admirable and unique design'; the beautiful fan tracery in the porches, vestry, and ground stage of the tower; the fine screen; fragments of contemporary glass, and other details, make it a notable example of Perpendicular work.

Modern brasses designed in fifteenth-century style have been placed in the indents of two missing female figures on a slab in the nave floor, traditionally said to be the burial-place of the Maids of Moreton, who founded the church. There is a mural tablet to a child of seven, daughter of Thomas Attenbury, who was 'Alderman of Buckingham and servant to King Charles II and King James'; and an eighteenth-century monument to Edward Bate and his wife. The Bates were a well-known local family, and Edward's father, Dr. George Bate, was physician successively to Charles I, Cromwell, and Charles II.

In the tower is the old oak door, pierced by a bullet, which is witness to the passing of the Parliamentarians in 1642, recorded at length in the church registers.

CHAPTER SIXTEEN: *Eastward from Aylesbury to the Bedfordshire Border*

AMONG the modern brick cottages and houses which are almost inevitable in a main road village, Bierton, which is only a mile and a half east of Aylesbury, has many thatched cottages and older houses clustering round its stately Perpendicular church, more than usually well worth a visit for its noble proportions and harmonious design. There is a good plain Norman font, and a small but attractive Jacobean monument to Samuel Bosse and his wife, with six children in cots below, and seven more behind them. A wall tablet commemorates Henry Peter Layard, the father of the explorer of Nineveh.

The church plate includes a rare and valuable fourteenth-century paten.

Two oval tablets commemorate Timothy Shaw and his wife, who died in 1786. Shaw was vicar of Bierton for thirty-four years, and preached so indefatigably in Bierton and neighbouring parishes that he was known as 'the Angel of the Seven Churches'. His son George, born in Bierton, was a distinguished naturalist, and Principal Keeper of Natural History in the British Museum.

Excavations at Bierton have yielded many relics of British and Roman times, coins of many periods, and also the bones of men and horses dating from the Civil War.

Just beyond Bierton a road branches off to Hulcott. The manor-house, church, a moated site shaded by lime-trees, and some very attractive cottages are set round an oval green. The manor-house has been modernized, but has a fine seventeenth-century staircase, with contemporary paintings from the stories of Phaedra and Hercules on the panels between the timber partitions of the wall.

There are no details earlier than the fourteenth century in the church, which has been thoroughly restored, and its chief interest is a rather distant connexion with the famous Brontës, whose uncle, William Morgan, was rector of Hulcott from 1851 to 1856. It was he who married Patrick Brontë to Maria Branwell, and was himself immediately afterwards married by Patrick Brontë to Maria's cousin Jane Fennell. Jane died before William Morgan came to Hulcott, and it is his second wife whose burial is recorded in the church register there.

At the Wingrave cross roads on the main road we can either turn south-east to Wingrave, or north-west to Aston Abbots.

Wingrave is on a low hill above the level meadows of the Vale of Aylesbury. The church is large, and mainly Perpendicular, but has twelfth-century wall-arcading in the chancel, a thirteenth-century vaulted chamber with contemporary wall-paintings, and numerous spiritedly carved corbels and capitals. The modern organ-case incorporates panels of about 1500, and there is seventeenth-century woodwork in the vestry. The rhymed record of Sir Richard Goddard's charity and some old books are also worth notice.

The custom of strewing hay or grass in the church is still observed on the first Sunday after St. Peter's Day (29 June).

William Wooley, who was vicar from 1753 to 1783, was a notorious 'witch-hunter' of his day. During his incumbency a poor old woman accused of bewitching her neighbour's spinning-wheel was stripped naked in the church and weighed on a pair of scales against the Church Bible. To the mortification of her accusers, she was found to outweigh the Bible, and triumphantly acquitted.

Aston Abbots was once a possession of the Abbots of St. Albans, who had their country seat there. The site is marked by a modern house, known as the Abbey, which was the home of Sir James Clark Ross, who made a number of voyages to the Arctic, and discovered the Magnetic Pole. He died at Aston Abbots in 1862, and is buried in the churchyard. There is a stained-glass window in the church to his memory. President Benes found a war-time home at the Abbey.

The church was entirely rebuilt in the nineteenth century, with the exception of the tower, but some of the fourteenth-century features were re-used. There are some charming walks in the neighbourhood.

The hamlet of Burston, or Birdstane, a mile from Aston Abbots, was mentioned in Domesday Book as Bricstock. Burston House was an old seat of the Lee family.

Wing lies just off the main road, at the meeting-place of a number of by-ways to secluded villages. It has many memories, and a Saxon church which must not be missed. Although the south aisle walls were rebuilt in the fourteenth century, the polygonal Saxon apse and the crypt are untouched. There are only eight Saxon crypts and four Saxon apses surviving in England to-day. The tower was added in the fourteenth century, and the clerestory in the following century.

The wealth of monuments and quaint inscriptions at Wing are chiefly to the Dormer family, who bought the manor in 1515. There are effigies of the Dormer husbands and wives, with their children, in a fine range of costumes, several brasses, including one to Thomas Cotes, porter to the Dormers at Ascott Hall, who died in 1648, with his high-crowned hat and a large key behind his kneeling figure, a porter's staff under his feet, and a quaint inscription. There is also a small Roubilliac to Lady Anne Sophia Dormer, daughter of the Earl of Carnarvon, and numerous interesting and attractive wall-tablets.

Dr. William Dodd, author of *The Beauties of Shakespeare*,

was vicar of Wing for two years before his death, though he never resided there. He was heavily involved in debt, and made various unsuccessful efforts to extricate himself, 'even descending so low as to become the editor of a newspaper'. Finally he was hanged at Tyburn for forgery. After what Lipscomb tactfully called his 'unfortunate death', Lord Chesterfield presented Henry Jerome de Salis, afterwards Count de Salis, to the living.

The home of the Dormers was half a mile east of Wing, and its site is marked by Ascott House. Princess Elizabeth is said to have slept there in 1544 on her way from Woodstock to Hampton Court, and Robert Dormer, who had been created Earl of Carnarvon, entertained Charles I for the night. One of the Royalist soldiers was hanged from a tree for stealing the Communion plate from the church. Three years later the mansion was sacked by Parliamentary troops. The Kennels of the Whaddon Chase Hunt were formerly at Ascott House. They are now at Wing.

There are some attractive sixteenth-century almshouses at Wing, and a number of old houses and cottages, considerably modernized. There are also numerous tumuli in the neighbourhood, and on Vicarage Farm is a large mound called Castle Hill, although no record of a castle has survived.

Scattered over the countryside which lies between the main road and the Chiltern hills are a number of villages which can only be reached by roundabout lanes. The nearest is Mentmore, on a hill commanding charming views. The picturesque mansion in its wide-spreading park was built by Sir Joseph Paxton, who designed the Crystal Palace. The church has been much restored, and has no monuments, but there are carved fifteenth-century angels in the roof. At a fifteenth-century restoration the piers of the nave were inverted, and the carved capitals now form the base of the pillars. In the grounds of Mentmore House there is a large

Stowe School

Wotton House

Newport Pagnell

Olney

statue of Favonius, the winner of the Derby in 1871, and the road to Cheddington runs through the Park.

Cheddington church has been restored, and is notable only for its charming view. Centuries of agriculture produced on the outlying chalk hills here the lynchets, or cultivation-terraces, which are especially noticeable on West End Hill. They originated when hillside fields were ploughed horizontally, with unploughed strips left at intervals. Their date is unknown.

We can make our way from Cheddington to Slapton, close to Bedfordshire, from which it is separated by the River Ousel. The little village lies between the river and the Grand Junction Canal, which has a lock and wharfage near the village. Decorated and Perpendicular arcades give an unexpectedly fine effect to the interior of the small church, which has brasses to Reginald Manser, a rector who died in 1462; Thomas Knyghton, in mass vestments, and to James Tornay, 'late Yeoman of the Crown to Kyng Henry the VIII'. John Kempe, who was rector until 1407, afterwards became Archbishop of York, then of Canterbury, and finally a Cardinal. He accompanied Henry V on the invasion of Normandy, and was on the Council of Henry VI.

Grove, which lies to the north of Slapton, was mentioned in Domesday Book. Although only two miles from Leighton Buzzard station, it remains almost incredibly secluded. The population has been less than twenty for at least half a century. The little church stands beside a lock on the Grand Junction Canal, and although now unimportant, and with no earlier work than the fourteenth century, has a Norman font. Traces of foundations discovered at the east end suggest there was once a larger Norman church.

Linslade is only separated from the Bedfordshire town of Leighton Buzzard by a narrow valley threaded by the railway, the Grand Junction Canal, and the River Ouzel.

New Linslade is a haunt of the hunting fraternity in winter, and the Hunt Hotel has some remarkable furniture made from the parts of a coach. Old Linslade lies apart, with its restored church neighboured by a Georgian manor-house, and the site of an old well which brought fame and prosperity in the thirteenth century, when Linslade became a market town and had a yearly fair lasting eight days. In 1299, however, the Bishop of Lincoln threatened to excommunicate any pilgrims to the Holy Well, and commanded the vicar of Linslade, who had accepted offerings, to appear before him. His prohibition appears to have brought Linslade's prosperity to an end, for there are no further references to the fair or market.

Linslade church was largely rebuilt in the fifteenth century. There is a beautiful thirteenth-century font and some small brasses of about 1500.

Many famous race-horses have been bred at the Rothschild stud farm at Southcote, a hamlet half a mile south-west of Linslade.

ii

Two roads running north-west from Linslade link up with all the villages of the Ouzel valley and those on the ridge of hills which runs north-west from Linslade to Whaddon Chase.

The first of these roads has a branch running to the Brickhills and Akeman Street, but we will continue on to Stoke Hammond, a pretty little village on a slope above the Grand Junction Canal and the Ouzel. The canal has a number of uncommonly handsome brick bridges, one of which is pictured on a modern window in the church.

The church dates from the middle of the fourteenth century, and has some fifteenth-century glass in a north window. The innumerable murals, chiefly to the Fountaine and the Disney families, are of various periods, but none of particular interest. John Chedworth was rector here in 1452, when he was elected Bishop of Lincoln, and John Hackett, who was rector between 1621 and 1624, was afterwards Bishop of Coventry and of Lichfield.

The two yew-trees in the churchyard were planted in 1687, and the Bell Inn also dates from the seventeenth century. Beyond Stoke Hammond is Newton Longueville, a large and attractive village which is growing increasingly popular as a residential centre for Bletchley. Nevertheless, in London End, Moor End, and Westbrook End the majority of the houses and cottages date from about 1575 to 1625, which seems to have been a special era of prosperity.

The manor-house, built at the beginning of the sixteenth century, incorporates part of the cell of the Benedictine Priory at Longueville in Normandy, from which Newton Longueville takes its name. There is a seventeenth-century shield over the doorway, with the arms of New College, Oxford, to whom it now belongs.

Browne Willis, writing in 1732, recorded that the gallows to which the lords of the manor had a right, still existed 'for peculiarity sake'. Possibly the Rev. William Cole, an eighteenth-century rector, wished it was also still in use, for in 1758, embittered by having to pay his predecessor's arrears of pension due to New College, he stigmatized Newton Longueville as 'a loose, disorderly, quarrelsome, litigious and drunken Place, and so noted in all the country'.

When the manor was granted to New College in 1441, for the rent of a red rose at Midsummer, the Norman church was largely rebuilt. Many alterations were also made in the nineteenth-century restoration, when, among other unfortunate mistakes, the twelfth-century font was decorated with modern carving. There is a modern brass to William Grocyn, who was rector from 1479 to 1504. He was the friend of Erasmus, and godfather to Lilly the grammarian, and himself one of the first teachers of Greek at Oxford University.

It is only two miles from Newton Longueville to Bletch-ley, but we will make our way north-west to Whaddon, which lies on a plateau nearly 500 feet high, and has some beautiful woods in the neighbourhood—all that survives of the great Whaddon Chase, where kings once hunted the wild boar. The Chase then covered over 2,000 acres and harboured 1,000 head of deer.

In the earlier centuries of its history Whaddon's lords of the manor were great personages, too busy playing their part in national history to visit this little manor, but Arthur, fourteenth Lord Grey de Wilton, took a liking to the place, greatly enlarged the original manor-house, and is said to have entertained Queen Elizabeth there. Much of this was pulled down when the manor was bought by the father of Browne Willis, but the antiquary partly rebuilt it. He lived there for fifty-six years until his death in 1760. In the garden was an ancient oak which Browne Willis cherished, believing that Spenser, who had been secretary to Lord Grey de Wilton, had written the *Faery Queene* in its shade. Near by is the moated site of the ancient priory of Snelshall.

The church is of all periods from Norman to Perpen-dicular. The Norman pillars with carved capitals of foliage and grotesque animals, the Early English font with the pulley for raising the cover, two oak alms-shovels, dated 1643, and several unusual and interesting monuments repay a visit to the church. One of the monuments is remarkable for a combination of brasswork and marble. Other brasses depict Margaret Missenden, who died in 1612, and her son in the form of a skeleton, and Amy Emerton, who gave a memorial clock to the church in 1612. A plain tomb under a canopy is the monument to the fourteenth Lord Grey de Wilton. He was appointed Lord Deputy of Ireland in 1580, and the inscription on his tomb relating his achievements tells us, 'he rooted out the traytors of the English pale' in that country. He returned to England in 1582, and spent the rest of his life at Whaddon, where he died in 1593. His son lost his estates for his participation in the Priest's Plot in James I's reign.

Three hundred and twenty ancient British gold coins were discovered in Whaddon Chase in 1849, and in an adjoining coppice are traces of a Roman camp enclosing about five acres.

Nash, which was at one time included with Whaddon, was made a separate parish in 1894, and has a small church designed by G. E. Street, of considerable interest to students of Victorian architecture.

From Whaddon or Nash we can make our way to Great Horwood and Little Horwood, which lie two and a half miles apart. Both have plenty of seventeenth-century cottages among their more modern houses, and there are a number more in the hamlet of Singleborough, north-west of Great Horwood, which has an inn called the 'Six Lords', a name which refers to the subdivision of the manor which took place in 1606.

Great Horwood church is Decorated and has a fine Perpendicular tower, but has been over-restored. There is a brass effigy of Henry Virgine, a fifteenth-century rector, in academical dress. His successor, William Warham, afterwards became Archbishop of Canterbury, and crowned Henry VIII and Catherine of Aragon in 1509. Joseph Spence, who became vicar of Great Horwood in 1742, was a friend of Pope, and the author of *Literary Anecdotes*.

Little Horwood church was originally built about 1200, but has been very much restored, and its most interesting feature is its series of wall-paintings. The picturesque little village has much half-timbering and thatch.

Mursley, now a small village of black-and-white cottages, was a market town in the thirteenth century, but its importance declined in the seventeenth century, with the passing of the Fortescue family, who built a magnificent mansion on the site of the old manor-house of the Fitz Niels, where they lived in great state. There is reason to believe they entertained Queen Elizabeth there in 1602, and James I and his queen certainly stayed at Salden House the following year, when twenty-two gentlemen were dubbed knights there on one June day.

The mansion was pulled down in the eighteenth century, a very small portion being incorporated into a farmhouse.

Mursley Hall dates from the seventeenth century, but has been modernized externally, and Manor Farm, on the east of the church, dates from the sixteenth century. The church stands on high ground, and is chiefly Decorated. It has a number of monuments to the Fortescues.

From Mursley we can either turn off to Drayton Parslow, or make our way direct to Stewkley. Drayton Parslow is a secluded little place with a fifteenth-century church restored and enlarged in the nineteenth century. Archdeacon Sharrock, son of Robert Sharrock, a seventeenth-century rector, was baptised in the church in 1630. He was the author of a *History of the Propagation and Improvement of Vegetables* and other works.

A mound half a mile south-west of the church may be the remains of a fortification thrown up by the Passelewes, who were lords of the manor in Norman times, and gave their name to the village.

The great attraction of Stewkley is its very beautiful Norman church, one of the best examples of its period in the kingdom, both in its massive structure and rich ornamentation. Doorways, windows, central tower arches—all are covered with a profusion of carving which has made the church justly famous.

The Earls of Gloucester and Cornwall held lands in Stewkley in Norman times, and they made grants to the abbey of Fontevrault. It was probably due to this connexion that the church was built on such a splendid plan.

From Stewkley we can turn south-west to Dunton, a church without a village, but neighboured by the rectory, a school, scattered houses, and an eighteenth-century manor-house, now a farm. The little church is worth visiting chiefly as an example of a typical country church of bygone days—nothing spectacular, yet wholly charming with its high pews, whitewashed ceilings, oak beams and an eighteenth-century gallery with painted texts, added when the collapse of the nave roof necessitated restoration.

Returning to the Stewkley road, we can either make our way back to Wing, or return by way of Soulbury, a small but very picturesque little village with a pond and green, two interesting manor-houses, and an impressive church with good Decorated and Perpendicular features, partly rebuilt in the early sixteenth century.

There are numerous memorials to the Lovetts, including a brass of 1491; an elaborate monument of Sir Robert Lovett, with the knight and his wife and children in early seventeenth-century costume; and an urn with cherubs and a palm by Grinling Gibbons. There are also some brasses.

South of the village, in a wide park, is Liscombe House, where the Lovetts have been seated from the thirteenth century. There has been a house there since at least 1250, but the present building dates from the sixteenth century. There are the remains of a fourteenth-century chapel, now connected with the house, in which marriages were celebrated before the alteration of the marriage laws, but which has since been used variously as a laundry, storehouse, and billiard-room. Chelmscott Manor, near the Grand Junction Canal, also has the remains of a fourteenth-century chapel which belonged to the house of the Lucys, long demolished. From Soulbury we can return direct to Linslade, or turn north along the Ouzel valley to Bletchley.

CHAPTER SEVENTEEN: *Watling Street*

THE modern town of Bletchley has grown up round the station, and is linked up with the modern development of Fenny Stratford, but the old village lies apart, half a mile west, with a fine avenue of ancient yews leading to its church.

Most of the older houses of Bletchley are thatched and half-timbered, and the church is Perpendicular, with a considerable amount of earlier work, and was 'repaired and beautified' early in the eighteenth century at the cost of Browne Willis, the antiquary who was then lord of the manor. The ceiling of the chancel was painted with figures of the twelve apostles.

There are some good monuments. Richard, Lord Grey de Wilton, who died in 1442, has an alabaster effigy of a man in plate armour; a delicately engraved brass to Dr. Thomas Sparke, a former rector, who died in 1616, depicts his portrait flanked by the figures of his three sons and two daughters, and those of his congregation, and above a quaint allegory with Death as a skeleton filling an urn from which Fame has seized the books written by the doctor—with all their titles clearly inscribed upon them. The coloured alabaster effigies of a man in sixteenth-century armour, and eight children, is said to have been brought by Browne Willis from Deptford church.

A fine copy of the 1638 Cambridge edition of the Bible, bound up with a Prayer Book and a metrical version of the Psalms said to have belonged to Charles I, was given to the church by Browne Willis.

Browne Willis inherited the Bletchley estate from his father in 1699. Both his parents were buried in the chancel of Bletchley church, and it was out of regard for their memory that he undertook the restoration of the church. He was a man of great industry, with a very retentive memory, and was one of the first antiquaries to base his works on the facts contained in records and registers. He took an active part in reviving the Society of Antiquaries in 1717, and was a voluminous writer on antiquarian subjects.

He was a man of great oddity of character, and through his generosity in building or repairing local churches, and his gifts to his children, he ruined himself, and 'was obliged to dress meanly and to live in squalor, becoming very dirty and penurious, so that he was often taken for a beggar'. His eccentricities were described in a poem by Dr. Darrell of Lillingstone Dayrell, and he is also mentioned by John Philips in his poem on *Cider*. He died in 1760, and was buried in Fenny Stratford.

Among the rectors presented by Browne Willis were Edward Wells, an eighteenth-century mathematician and geographer, and William Cole, the antiquary and friend of Horace Walpole, whose unique collection of MSS. is now in the British Museum.

Although, as its name of 'Strat' or 'Stret' implies, Fenny Stratford is on the Roman Watling Street, and of ancient origin, the site of the Roman station of Magiovintum was south of the modern town. A weekly market was granted in 1204, and it was mentioned under the name of Fenni Stratford as early as 1252, when an annual fair was granted; in 1347 a royal writ issued to the sheriff of the county ordered him to build as many bridges from Leighton Buzzard to Fenny Stratford as used to be there, which points to considerable traffic on the road. It had attained to borough status by 1370, and grew in importance until the disastrous effects of the Civil War, which led to the destruction of the church and the lapse of the market, checked its prosperity. In 1665 there was a terrible visitation of the plague, when the road was temporarily diverted and the inns closed. In spite of the efforts of Browne Willis, it did not recover its prosperity until modern times. A diary of 1768 referred to it as 'a very small disunited village, not sufficiently considerable to deserve observation'.

The mellow red-brick church was built largely at the expense of Browne Willis, but the arms of the other contributors ornament the ceiling of the north aisle. Curiously enough, both the father and the grandfather of Dr. Willis died on St. Martin's Day (11 November), and the latter died at his house in St. Martin's Lane, London. The church is dedicated to St. Martin, and Dr. Willis instituted the custom of firing salvoes from six quaint little pieces of ordnance, known as Fenny Poppers, in memory of his parents. The custom is still continued. Divine service is held in the church in the morning, and a dinner in the evening. An inscription in Latin on Browne Willis's tomb in the church also pays tribute to the memory of his famous grandfather, author of numerous brilliant medical treatises.

Little Brickhill, which lies about two miles south of Fenny Stratford, on a hill beside Watling Street, was once a place of considerable importance as a convenient stage for travellers. It is possible it was a borough by the thirteenth century. It certainly had a market and fair by that time. There is mention of the assembly of commissioners for gaol delivery about 1284, and from 1433 to 1638 the assizes and other county meetings were held there. The church registers contain the names of forty-two people who 'suffered death and were buried' between the years 1561 and 1618, presumably in connexion with the assizes.

The old assize house was newly fronted in modern times, and only one of the many ancient inns survives. The church is chiefly Perpendicular, restored in the Victorian era. In the churchyard, near the south porch, is a tombstone inscribed, 'Here lieth the body of True Blue', who died in 1724, and of whom nothing further is known.

The Roman station of Magiovintum was at Dropshort, a hamlet which lies on Watling Street between Little Brickhill and Fenny Stratford. Excavations made in 1911 yielded interesting finds.

An old rhyme says:

Here stand three Brickhills all in a row
Great Brickhill, Little Brickhill, and Brickhill of the Bow.

The name is possibly derived from the British word 'brik', an earlier form of the Welsh 'brig', meaning top or summit. Great Brickhill, the largest of the three, is yet the most secluded, reached down a country road bordered with pine-woods, and set on a sandy ridge commanding wide views. The restored church is mainly Perpendicular, with many monuments to the Duncombe family, who have been lords of the manor since 1549. Brickhill Manor is a modern house on an ancient site, in a large park. There are many charming seventeenth-century houses and cottages in the village. William Peirce, a nephew of the famous Hugh Peters who was associated with Winthrop in the founding of Massachusetts, was rector of Great Brickhill from 1656 to the Restoration.

Bow Brickhill, right on the Bedfordshire border, is high on a sandy, pine-clad ridge with its church 100 feet higher, on the top of the hill, and a landmark for many miles. The prefix Bow first appeared in 1198 as Bolle, and was probably the name of a one-time tenant. There are some attractive old houses in the village, and the Wheatsheaf Inn is a thatched, half-timbered building dating from about 1600. The church was completely remodelled and thoroughly restored by Browne Willis. The font and pulpit date from the fifteenth century, and there is a monument to William Watson, 'of yeoman race', who was 'parson of this church full thirty and six years' and died in 1608, 'in the sixth yeare of the happy reigne of Kinge James over England'. Thomas Webster's painting of a Village Choir, now in the Sheepshank Collection, Victoria and Albert Museum, was painted in Bow Brickhill church, but the gallery and other details are imaginative.

There is no village actually on Watling Street between Fenny Stratford and Stony Stratford, although Shenley Church End and Loughton are close by. Shenley church is on a hill overlooking Church End, and the charming little Shenley Brook End a mile away. The fine church has all periods since 1150 blended into a harmonious whole, and two good monuments: one, dated 1607, to Thomas Stafford, who died at the age of eighty, to whom Shenley owes its attractive little almshouses; and another to Sir Edmund Ashfyld, who died in 1577, and his wife, with a delicately ornamented pediment on which are some lion heads. About a quarter of a mile south-west of the church is the Toot, a mound with two large moated enclosures, covering about seven acres, in one of which are traces of the foundations of the old manor-house of Shenley, pulled down in 1774. Part of a Roman tessellated pavement and Roman bricks were found at Dovecot Farm, Brook End, in 1901.

Loughton, on the north of Watling Street, is an attractive mingling of old and new houses, with a church dating from the early thirteenth century, although much altered in later centuries. The unusually interesting manor-house, originally built in 1500, was beautifully restored in the present century. It has some curious sixteenth-century mural paintings. The church has a sixteenth-century brass and a number of seventeenth-century monuments. An iron-bound poorbox dates from the sixteenth century, and there are two grotesquely carved wood panels, and fragments of old glass. A painting by the eighteenth-century Spanish artist Gonzales was given to the church by the Rev. John Athawes on his induction to the living in 1833.

Set on Watling Street where it crosses the River Ouse,

Stony Stratford is almost encircled by the river, which here forms the county boundary. Although situated on the Roman Watling Street, modern research seems to prove it was not a Roman station, but it has been a market town and a haunt of travellers since very early times.

King John was at Stony Stratford in 1215, and Henry IV in 1409, as shown by documents dated there; Shakespeare reminds us in *Richard III* that Edward V slept there on his way up to London, and that his half-brother, Lord Grey, and others of his relatives and friends, were arrested there on the orders of the Duke of Gloucester. Margaret of Scotland dated a letter from there in 1516, and Henry VIII received a Hungarian Embassy there in 1531; and in 1540 there is a record that one of the tapsters following in the train of the Court was condemned for profiteering on victuals to sit in the pillory of the town.

Its greatest period of prosperity began with the coaching era, when it had many famous inns catering for those who travelled to Ireland by way of Chester. The most celebrated was the Cock, first mentioned in 1500, which still survives, although rebuilt. The Bull is another old inn still to be seen, and these two are traditionally those where the fantastic tales of travellers gave rise to the phrase 'a cock and bull story'. Some of the earlier inn-keepers were by no means the 'jolly host' of fiction—one in 1596 was stigmatized as 'a notable bad fellow', and other tales were current.

The town saw much coming and going in the Civil War, when the Earl of Cleveland maintained a station there for the King, but it had the good fortune to remain 'a populous and much frequented market town', suffering little, apart from the destruction of the Eleanor Cross, erected by Edward I. Two great fires in the eighteenth century did far more damage, sweeping away many of the older houses, and apparently destroying its character, for a writer then described it as 'a small straggling town, not remarkable in any shape'. As late as 1819 a visitor complained that it was 'most vilely paved'.

Nonconformists were very active at Stony Stratford in the seventeenth century, and several Quakers were arrested for attempting to hold a meeting in 1661, but in 1672 a house was licensed for Presbyterian worship. Wesley is said to have preached under the elm-tree in the market-place.

During the same period Thomas Smith was arrested on suspicion of being a Jesuit, and in 1666 the house of John Digby, son of the famous Sir Kenelm Digby, was searched and 300 arms found. Although they were not taken away, so far from being thankful to escape arrest, 'he took it so ill that he went away in his coach and six horses'.

Only the Perpendicular tower of St. Mary's remains, the church never having been rebuilt. St. Giles's church also has its original Perpendicular tower. The remainder of the church was reconstructed in 1776, but unfortunately spoiled in the Victorian era by incongruous fittings.

Apart from some very attractive houses built since the eighteenth-century fires, and one or two older buildings which escaped being burned, Stony Stratford has comparatively few tangible relics of its long history, but it has much charm, and many odd corners to reward the seeker after the picturesque. The complicated design on the eighteenth-century wrought-iron bracket on which the sign of the Bull Inn swings is worth notice.

Wolverton, two miles to the north-east, on the road to Newport Pagnell, has an old and a new town. Mentioned in Domesday Book, the old town then had two mills, one of which probably stood on the same site as the present-day mill beside the Ouse. Soon afterwards it had a castle and church, and was the head of the large barony of Manno the Breton. The site of the castle keep can still be seen in the grounds of Holy Trinity church, and the moat, filled in when the new church was built, can be traced on the south of the vicarage, but there is no record of its history. As early as 1248 there was a manor-house with a garden. It was rebuilt in the fifteenth century by the Longville family, but it was pulled down in 1720. The vicarage was built out of some of the material.

The church, approached down the vicarage drive, has a fourteenth-century tower, the rest of the structure dating from 1815, when it was rebuilt in a costly style which excited the admiration of Lipscomb. Coloured decorations were added in 1877. A huge marble monument commemorated Sir Thomas Longville of Wolverton, the second baronet, who died in 1685.

New Wolverton originated with the establishment there of the London and North-Western Railway engine-works in 1838, and has all the advantages—and drawbacks—of its origin. Ample employment and social amenities provided by the railway company are offset by the usual concomitants of industrial development in the Victorian era.

THE country north of Watling Street, with its typically English charm of rich meadows, innumerable placid little streams, and backwaters gay with water-lilies and yellow iris, and its quiet towns and villages, is an unknown land to the majority of people in South Bucks, owing to the difficulty of access. There is no through bus, coach, or railway service between south and north beyond Aylesbury.

Londoners are in a different category—all the railways serving North Bucks have direct trains from the metropolis, yet for some happy reason the far north of the county has never been spoiled by undiscriminating development, and remains the quiet agricultural district it has been since the earliest times.

New Wolverton and New Bradwell are now joined up along the Newport Pagnell road, and the newer part of Stantonbury merges with both, but Old Bradwell lies a mile south, and the disused church of Stantonbury lies apart as Stanton Low on the other side of the River Ouse.

The Early English church at Old Bradwell has been too zealously restored, but has the remains of thirteenth-century inscriptions on the chancel arch, some fragments of old glass, and two of the five known bells of Michael de Wymbis. On the north-west of the village is Moat House, which was formerly the manor-house. A quiet country lane dips under the railway and leads to Bradwell Abbey, which was built out of the ruins of a Benedictine monastery in the seventeenth century, and is now a farmhouse. There are the remains of a moat, and of the priory fish-ponds, and a small chapel dating in part from the twelfth century, now a farm-store. It has eighteenth-century paintings on the ceiling showing angels blowing trumpets against a blue sky with pink, yellow, and grey clouds.

On the north-east of the village are traces of a small mound and bailey castle, of whose history nothing is known. It may have been thrown up during the reign of Stephen.

Stantonbury, which originated in Saxon times, had declined to four houses in 1736, but the small, towerless church, with its magnificently carved Norman chancel arch, still stands beside the Ouse, and was restored in 1910.

Within a mile of Stantonbury church, on the road to Gayhurst, is Haversham, a rather straggling village with a church containing much Norman work. A monument of exceptional splendour has the recumbent effigy of an unknown lady. Modern authorities consider the tomb to be of late fourteenth-century work. There are two brasses, and some old glass and woodwork. There is also some good glass dating from 1850. In one of the modern windows John the Baptist is portrayed with six toes on one foot!

Lipscomb pays tribute to Edward Cooke, who was rector of Haversham from 1802 to 1824, saying he was 'an assiduous collector of books and manuscripts relative to the history of his native county, of which, by his generous beneficence, the writer has so largely availed himself in the compilation of this work'.

The seventeenth-century manor-house has the remains of a moat and a seventeenth-century dovecote. Eighteenth-century alterations to the manor-house were presumably the work of Alexander Small, described in a contemporary record as 'a great Sportsman and much given up to amorous Dalliance, as reported, so as to occasion great Uneasiness at Home'.

Haversham Grange, which lies about a quarter of a mile north-east of the church, is an early seventeenth-century gabled house, with fourteenth-century details which are probably survivals from the grange of the Abbot of Lavendon on the same site.

Returning to the Newport Pagnell road, by way of Little
Linford, charmingly set above the lush water-meadows of
the Ouse valley, we find a small church with a thirteenth-
century bell-turret and an ancient font; and an old Hall.
There was a bridge across the Ouse here before the fourteenth century. Great Linford, which lies south of the Newport Pagnell road, is a peaceful and charming place, in spite
of the close proximity of the main road, railway, and the
Grand Junction Canal. It appears in history as early as 944,
when King Edmund gave it to his thegn Ælfhead, and the
present church dates from 1250, though so extensively
enlarged and altered in later centuries that little of the
original character is left. There are some Georgian box
pews and other wooden fittings, and interesting brasses
and inscriptions. An eighteenth-century monument commemorates Sir William Pritchard, who was 'Alderman, and
sometime since Lord Mayor of London. . . . He was one of
the City's Representatives in sevl. Parliaments, and President of St. Bartholomew's Hospital, where he erected a
convenient apartment for cutting of the stone; and built and
endowed a School House and Six Alms Houses in this
Parish.'

The almshouses and schoolhouse Sir Thomas Pritchard
built still stand near Great Linford church, and there are
some other ancient buildings, including the Old Wharf Inn,
and an elegant eighteenth-century manor-house at Linford
Wharf.

Newport Pagnell, set where the River Lovat, or Ouzel,
joins the Ouse, at the meeting-place of several important
roads, was 'New' before the time of Domesday Book, in
which it is described as a borough, and took the name of
Pagnell from its Norman lords, the Paynel or Painel family.
It had two bridges from the earliest years of its history, and
there are many references to repairs carried out from 1187
onwards.

Only the site remains of the Norman castle, the memory of which is preserved in a meadow which has been known as Castle Mead since the twelfth century. The Norman church was rebuilt in the fourteenth century; and the surviving fragments of the Norman Tickford Abbey were built into the walls of a modern mansion perpetuating its name. Yet so gently has time dealt with the town since the end of the Civil War that it remains the very picture of old-world charm, rich in seventeenth- and eighteenth-century buildings, and very full of interesting associations.

The modern St. John's Hospital, originally founded in 1240, has a beam from the seventeenth-century rebuilding with the inscription: 'Alyou good Chrystianes that heere dooe pas by give soome thynge to thes poor people that in St. John's Hospital doeth ly. Ano. 1615.' Three of the inns —the King's Arms, the Swan, and the George—are old, and some of the street and place names give the clue to former buildings of the town and neighbourhood.

Newport had several royal visits in the thirteenth century; Cromwell stayed there in 1644, and later in the same year his son Oliver, who was described by a contemporary as 'a civil young gentleman, and the joy of his father', died there of small-pox when serving with the Parliamentary garrison who had supplanted the Royalists. The Governor of the town at that time was Sir Samuel Luke, who is believed to have been the original of Butler's *Hudibras*.

The large and beautiful Decorated church of Newport Pagnell is set on a slight rise above the River Lovat. The nave has a richly moulded early sixteenth-century roof supported on stone angel corbels, and decorated with carved figures of angels and saints. There is a fifteenth-century brass; numerous wall tablets; two chained books; an iron-bound chest dating from about 1600 with incised panels; and a richly carved chest of about 1650; and other interesting features. The north porch has a Priest's Chamber over it.

In the beautiful churchyard sloping down to the river is the tomb of Thomas Abbot Hamilton, who died in 1788, at the age of thirty-two, with an epitaph by Cowper, who was a friend of his brother-in-law, Dr. Greatheed.

John Gibbs, who was vicar during the Commonwealth, was ejected at the Restoration, and became the first Non-conformist minister of the town. When he died in 1699 he was so greatly respected that the deeds of the Baptist meeting-house at Olney expressly mentioned, 'no person shall ever be chosen pastor, who shall differ in his religious sentiments from the Rev. John Gibbs of Newport Pagnell'. There is an altar tomb to his memory in the parish church. The Independent Meeting-House, which stands near Gibbs's original meeting-house, has several memorials to early Non-conformists, including one to the Rev. William Bull, a friend of Cowper, who was pastor from 1764 until his death in 1814. His *Life* was written by his son, Josiah, who succeeded him as pastor, but he is perhaps best known from Cowper's tribute, 'He was a Dissenter, a liberal one, a man of letters and genius, master of a fine imagination, a man of erudition and ability'. A fragment of a pulpit used by John Bunyan is preserved in the chapel.

ii

Broughton, on the Woburn road, is near the Bedford-shire border, and has assimilated some of the character of a Bedfordshire village. The small fourteenth-century church has two old books chained to desks on either side of the chancel arch, and there are fragments of fourteenth-century glass, but interest centres in the remarkable series of paintings on the walls of the nave.

Down a lane south-west of Broughton is the pretty little village of Milton Keynes, with a seventeenth-century inn, and one of the finest Decorated churches in the county. There is a brass of a priest, some encaustic tiles, and a chained

Bible. In a field to the west of the church are the remains of a moat and traces of fishponds, which probably mark the site of the ancient manor-house.

The rectory was built by Dr. William Wotton, the antiquary, who was rector from 1693 to 1726. He was the friend of Sir Isaac Newton, and author of *Reflections on Ancient and Modern Learning*, which roused Swift to write his *Battle of the Books*. Wotton could read a psalm at the age of four years, Latin when five, and Hebrew a few months later! In the earlier rectory on the site, Francis Atterbury, the famous Jacobite Bishop of Rochester, was born. His father, Lewis Atterbury, author of *Babylon's Downfall*, was rector from 1657 to his death in 1693.

Moulsoe, which lies on a by-way north of Broughton, is a charming village on high ground commanding wide views. The large church has been almost rebuilt in modern times. There is a brass, lacking its inscription, a few old monuments, a chest dating from 1300, four seventeenth-century coffin stools, and an unusually fine oaken coffin bier, dated 1651.

Wavendon, farther south along the main road, has a conspicuous church which almost lost its original character at the restoration in 1849, and has become an unusually fine example of a good type of Victorian interior, with one of the largest collections of Victorian glass in Bucks. The pulpit is said to have been brought from the church of St. Dunstan-in-the-West, London, and the carving is attributed to Grinling Gibbons. The manor-house and a number of houses in the village date from the seventeenth century. The fuller's earth pits of the neighbourhood were said in 1578 to be 'very profitable and commodious for fulling'.

In the seventeenth and eighteenth centuries Wavendon included the district called Hogsty End, now Woburn Sands, which was one of the most important centres of the Quakers.

A country lane runs west to Walton, in the valley of the Lovat, whose modern name of Ouzel bids fair to supplant the name which has endured since at least 1200. Church and manor-house neighbour each other in the water-meadows—completely charming and isolated, for a mere handful of cottages and two farms make up the village. The church is a mixture of styles from the fourteenth century onwards. A brass commemorates an eleven-year-old child who died in 1617, with a long inscription. There is also a medallion by Nollekens to Sir Thomas Pinfold, king's advocate and Chancellor of Peterborough, who died in 1701, with a record of his achievements, and another to Charles Pinfold, Governor of Barbadoes, who died in 1788. There is also a small but notable seventeenth-century monument with two marble busts to Bartholomew Beale and 'Katharine his only wife'. It was erected by their son, Charles Beale, of Walton Manor, whose wife Mary was one of the best female portrait painters of the day. A number of her portraits, including one of Charles II, are in the National Portrait Gallery. Her husband's diaries, now in the British Museum, contain full details of her life and work.

A return to Newport Pagnell can be made up the Ouzel valley, visiting several interesting villages on the way. Simpson, five miles from Newport Pagnell, has a Decorated church with memorials to the Hamner family.

The road runs north from Simpson between the canal and river to Woughton-on-the-Green. The green has disappeared, but the church, seventeenth-century inn, and half-timbered houses survive, with an older, moated building near the canal. The thirteenth-century church was enlarged in the following century. It has a fourteenth-century effigy of a priest resting his feet on a dog, eighteenth-century murals, an impressive Royal Arms of William IV, and interesting Communion plate.

Great Woolstone belies its name by having only a few

houses, but those all extremely decorative and dating from the seventeenth century. The church was rebuilt in 1839 on an earlier site. Weeden Butler the younger, who contributed to Nichol's *Literary Anecdotes*, was rector from 1816 to 1831. His brother, the Rev. George Butler, was Headmaster of Harrow.

The cottages of Little Woolstone lie back from the road along a lane leading to a seventeenth-century farm and mill-house, and a fourteenth-century church with a curious bell-cote constructed of ancient timbers covered with modern weather-boards. There is a Norman font and fragments of fourteenth-century glass, but as a whole the interior is more Victorian than Decorated. Dorothy Wyndlow Pattison, better known for her philanthropic work as Sister Dora, was schoolmistress at Little Woolstone from 1861 to 1864, before joining the Sisterhood of the Good Samaritan at Redcar.

The last village before reaching Newport Pagnell is Willen, whose church, long thought to be the work of Wren, was designed by his pupil, Dr. Robert Hooke, in 1678, and built at the expense of Dr. Busby, the famous headmaster of Westminster School, in whose house Hooke had lodged as a boy. There are numerous entries in Hooke's diary relating to the planning and building of the church. The rectory is approached by an avenue of limes from the church. The old rectory was designed to match the church, but was destroyed by fire in 1947, together with the library presented to the church by Dr. Busby and a later donor.

iii

There are some very distinguished villages on the North-ampton road. Lathbury, just over the Ouse from Newport Pagnell, though only small, has a notable church in the park of the mansion built in 1801 on the site of the old home of the Andrewes family. The church dates from the early twelfth century, and has many interesting details, including an early twelfth-century carved tympanum reset in the wall of the south aisle; carved capitals on the late twelfth-century arcade, depicting dragons feeding on foliage; traces of fifteenth-century wall-paintings; and some interesting monuments and inscriptions. A brass to Richard Davies of Kynant, Montgomeryshire, who died in 1661, has an inscription:

'He deceased at the house of his son Isaiah Davies, then minister of this parish, 20th day of November 1661, aged 77 years. His son Thomas Davies, Esq., at that time Agent Generall for the English nation upon the coast of Africa caused a scenotaph to be erected in the church of Welch Poole, the place of his birth, to the pious memory of his father, and this small memorial for such Cambria-Brittaines as shall this way travaile.'

There is also an inscription to Margaret Andrewes, daughter of the lord of the manor, who died in 1680 at the age of fourteen. She left a bequest to pave the church with slabs of black and white marble, some of which have since been utilized as memorials to other members of the Andrewes family. Her cousin, Elizabeth, who was married at the age of sixteen years to Lord Leigh, and died after an unhappy married life at the age of twenty-seven, is buried in the chancel. The manor passed in the female line after the death of Henry Andrewes in 1744. His daughter, Jane Symes, was a redoubtable lady who defied the Duke of Cumberland in her Jacobite zeal, and refused to open a gate and private bridge on her estate to allow him passage when on his way to fight Bonnie Prince Charlie.

Tyringham, which lies down a lane north of the main road, consists solely of a perfectly grouped and designed gateway, house, and church approached by a graceful bridge across the Ouse, which flows through the park. All but the church were designed by Sir John Soane in 1793 and are superb examples of his art, unaltered except for the addition of a dome and balustrade to the house, and gardens designed by Lutyens.

The lower stages of the church date from the twelfth century and the bell-chamber from about 1500, the rest having been rebuilt in 1871. There are two brasses to members of the Tyringham family, who held the manor for 400 years. Most of the few parishioners live at Filgrave, which lies nearly two miles north-east, near Filgrave church, which fell into disuse in the seventeenth century.

Only the road and river separate Tyringham from Gayhurst Park, where again there is a splendid house and church and no village. The Elizabethan mansion was begun by Sir Everard Digby, who became fatally involved in the Gunpowder Plot and suffered a terrible death in expiation, leaving his young widow to bring up his two sons, John, who was killed at the Battle of Langport in 1645, fighting for the son of the King who had executed his father, and Sir Kenelm, who lived to become one of the most handsome, charming, and gifted men of his age, and whom Sir Thomas Browne called 'this Magazine of all the Arts' and 'the Ornament of England'. He is said to have imported from the South of France the large edible snail *Helix pomatia*, for the benefit of his wife Venetia, who was consumptive. They still abound in the woods of Gayhurst. There is a priest's hiding-place known as Digby's Hole, said to have been constructed by Sir Everard Digby, and a yew walk in the garden is known as Digby's Walk. One of the rooms is covered with seventeenth-century hand-painted leather ornamented with designs of peacocks, parrots, and other birds, and in the grounds is a pedestal with some lines *To the Memory of a Beautifully Mottled Peacock*.

Gayhurst was bought in 1704 by George Wright, son of Lord Keeper Nathan Wright, and father of the George Wright who rebuilt the medieval church in 1728. There are numerous monuments in the church to the Wright family, the earliest of which is by Roubilliac to Lord Keeper Wright and his son. William Unwin Cowper visited Gayhurst, and wrote: 'I was delighted at all I found there. The situation is happy, the gardens elegantly disposed; the hothouse in the most flourishing state, and the orange trees the most captivating creations of the kind I ever saw.'

There are roads from Gayhurst to Hanslope and Castlethorpe on the Northamptonshire border. Hanslope is set on high ground, and has more the character of a Midland village than one in the Buckinghamshire tradition. The church has a chancel dating from about 1160, with north and south aisles added in the thirteenth century and a magnificent tower in the fifteenth century. The spire is modern, and a very conspicuous object in a county not noted for spires. There are several brasses, including one to a child who died in 1602, and another to the parents of Richard Troughton, with an inscription 'composed in duetye by their beeloved Sonne'. There are traces of fifteenth-century wall-paintings, and good carved stone-work, including fine gargoyles on the exterior. In the churchyard is the tomb of Joseph Cox, who died in 1759, at the age of ninety-two, and his wife, who died in 1762, at the age of 101, leaving 174 living descendants, and a pathetic epitaph to Alexander M'Kay, of Glasgow, a famous prize-fighter who died in 1830, aged twenty-six. Only the earthworks now remain of Hanslope Castle, which was sacked and destroyed in 1215. Castle Hill, where it stood, is on the north of the neighbouring village of Castlethorpe. The fortified manor-house which succeeded it has also disappeared, but part of the neighbouring mansion-house occupied by Sir Peter Tyrell in 1703 is incorporated in the building known as Castle Yard. Silver armlets showing late Celtic influence, and Roman coins, have been found at Castlethorpe. The church, close to Castle Hill, has some late twelfth-century work. The tower was rebuilt in the eighteenth century, when the earlier one fell down. There is a carved fourteenth-century font, and a large monument to Sir Thomas Tyrell, Justice of the Court of Common Pleas, who died in 1671.

Stoke Goldington, the last village before the road crosses the border into Northamptonshire, lies in an upland hollow. The church is on a hill a quarter of a mile away, neighboured by a seventeenth-century farmhouse much altered in later periods, which was originally the manor-house. The church, without being of special interest, is large and handsome, and the village has substantial cottages, a gabled seventeenth-century house, and a school, so that it would appear it has improved since one of its ministers wrote in 1773: 'The country is pleasant; the villages large and populous; but the people poor, ignorant, and idle. The highest wages of the labourer in harvest time is only 1s. 6d. per day without meat. Half the inhabitants have little more knowledge, save the art of lacemaking, than they were born with. There are no schools for the poor, and they have no means of instruction but at church, where the greater part never come. Those that have any religion are almost all Methodists and fanatics of one sort or another. Taking the whole county, I think it remarkably poor and ignorant.'

iv

Before finally setting out for Olney, we can follow the Bedford road to the county boundary to see a little group of villages. Chicheley, two miles from Newport Pagnell on the main road, in a hollow shaded by trees, is a picturesque place where the traveller may well linger with advantage. The church combines alterations of nearly every period since the original twelfth-century building. The eighteenth-century work is especially effective. There are some good brasses, including one to Anthony Cave, who died in 1560, depicting a shrouded skeleton and the Cave arms, with an inscription, which is curiously repeated on the monument to the same Anthony Cave which was erected by his widow in 1576. There is also a large seventeenth-century monument to Sir Anthony Chester and his wife, and other elaborate eighteenth-century marble murals to members of the Chester family.

Near the church is the mansion which replaced the Tudor manor of the Caves. Built about 1701, it well deserves the praise of Lloyd in the *History of English Brickwork*. Set in extensive grounds, it is a splendid combination of architectural design, fine workmanship, and rich texture, although its architect is not known. It was here that Cowper had a memorable day's outing to visit his friend Charles Chester, which he described in a letter to Lady Hesketh in November 1787.

Among the many farms of the parish is Balney Lodge, or Grange Farm, which has an Elizabethan south wing and an eighteenth-century east wing, and is identified with the ancient manor-house of the Broughtons. The modern Thickthorn Farm has traces of old fish-ponds and an old homestead moat. There is an Elizabethan gabled house and some seventeenth-century half-timbered cottages with thatched roofs in the hamlet of Bedlam.

North Crawley, south-east of Chicheley, should not be missed. Its large and handsome church contains a considerable amount of early woodwork, including an unusually interesting example of a late fifteenth-century rood-screen with painted panels. A brass of 1548 to Robert Latimer and his wife and daughter has an ungrammatical inscription, and another to a former rector, John Garbrand, who died in 1589, has a black-letter inscription.

The Grange, a quarter of a mile north-east of the church, is a much-restored Tudor house. The royal arms, with the Tudor rose above and the Plantagenet portcullis below, carved on one of the oak window shutters, is probably a relic of the visit of Queen Elizabeth in 1575. The old seventeenth-century manor-house, which is surrounded by a moat and is now partly ruined, stands in the hamlet of East End, on the site of Hollowes Manor in Great Crawley, and Moat Farm, an early sixteenth-century house at Little Crawley, was probably the manor-house of Pateshull, or Little Crawley Manor.

Astwood, which lies on either side the Bedford road, close to the county boundary, can be reached direct from North Crawley. Its church was damaged by bombs in the 1939–45 war. It should be visited for its spirited eighteenth-century monuments, one of which commemorates the son of 'Ways and Means' Lowndes of Winslow. There are one or two brasses, a fourteenth-century font, and sixteenth- and seventeenth-century woodwork.

The small village round the green has a number of thatched cottages. The Manor Farm marks the site of the old manor-house, and a moat and dove-house are all that remain of the great mansion of Astwood Bury. The dove-house has been converted into a cottage. Returning along the main road to its junction with the Olney road, a lane on the left can be taken to Hardmead, a restored village in an agricultural parish. The small church, originally built about 1250, has fragments of the ancient glass, fifteenth-century seats and two desk-fronts, a fine oak bier dated 1670, and a fifteenth-century octagonal font to offset the fittings added at the Victorian restoration.

There is a well-drawn brass effigy of Francys Catesby, who died in 1556. A conspicuous monument to a later Francis Catesby, who died in 1636, shows him with the kneeling figures of his son and two daughters in a recess built up in the likeness of piles of books. There are numerous other monuments to the Catesby family, who held the manor from the fifteenth to the seventeenth century, but whose house has completely disappeared, though its moated site can still be seen on the north of the church.

A large marble tablet on the north wall of the chancel commemorates Robert Shedden, who sailed in his yacht *Nancy Dawson*, pictured on the monument, to search for Sir John Franklin, the Arctic explorer, and 'drooped and died on the dark blue sea on board his yacht'. He was buried in the Protestant burial-ground at Mazatlan, in the Pacific, in 1849. The Sheddens' are still lords of the manor.

v

Sherington, which is passed soon after turning into the Olney road, has the older part of the village clustering round the church almost undisturbed, whilst the newer part borders the highway. The older and higher end of the village has been known as Church End since the sixteenth century, and is dominated by the church, an imposing building more suggestive of Northamptonshire than of Bucks. There is a late fourteenth-century font, but the fittings are chiefly modern.

Emberton, the only other village on the main road before reaching Olney, is set above the River Ouse, and commands a view of the spire of Olney church rising from its surrounding trees. The centre of the village is dignified by a mid-nineteenth-century clock-tower, and the spacious Decorated church is on high ground to the south-west. The tower is particularly fine. The windows contain some of the richest Decorated tracery in Bucks, and the external wall of the chancel has a cornice of flowers and grotesques.

There is a carved font dating from about 1400, and a fifteenth-century brass showing a priest in mass vestments, with a long inscription in Latin, and a scroll issuing from his mouth inscribed, 'Jon preyth the sey for hym a pater noster & an ave'.

CHAPTER NINETEEN: Cowper's Country

THE long bridge across the Ouse to Olney which Cowper knew was rebuilt in 1832, and there have been many other changes since the poet's day, but happily much remains, and for all its modernisation, Olney seems permeated with the spirit of the gentle, lovable man who made it famous.

Even in the present day, the Ouse is liable to flood the meadows around Olney in the rainy season, giving colour to the belief that the name is derived from the Old English 'Olla's Island'. Although Olney is mentioned in Domesday Book, had a market by 1205, and was a borough by 1237, it seems to have been one of those rare places which have been happy in having no history. Cowper, and in a lesser degree his friend Newton, with whom he wrote the *Olney Hymns*, lure the traveller to Olney to recapture the atmosphere described in the correspondence of Cowper, justly called by Southey 'the best of English letter-writers'.

Not only the town and its surroundings, but its everyday life, are so vividly portrayed that the veriest stranger arriving in Olney must needs feel it peopled with old friends. Cowper's house is now a museum of relics, and in the garden behind is still to be found the little summer-house he described in a letter to Joseph Hill: '. . . not much bigger than a sedan chair, the door of which opens into the garden, that is now crowded with pinks, roses and honeysuckles, and the window opening into my neighbour's orchard . . . here I write all that I write in summer-time, whether to my friends, or to the public . . .' It was in this little summer-house that Cowper wrote the immortal *John Gilpin*, and most of *The Task*.

Quotations from Cowper's letters and poems crowd upon the mind when writing of Olney, but it is best left to the reader to browse through his gossiping pages, and re-live those far-off days with Cowper himself. All the material is at hand in his letters.

In the eighteenth-century vicarage is the study in which Newton wrote *The Letters of Omicron* and *Cardiphonia*, and over the mantelpiece are the texts he had painted there. He entertained a distinguished circle of friends, and it was in this house that Thomas Charles of Bala, the organizer of Welsh Calvinistic Methodism, met the leading Nonconformists of the day, whilst on a summer vacation.

The labours of both Newton and Cowper in the cause of Nonconformity are well known. Olney was also the scene of the work of John Sutcliff, one of the founders of the Baptist Missionary Society, who in 1799 established a seminary for training missionaries in the premises which are now No. 23 High Street, Olney. William Carey, the orientalist and missionary, another of those who worked for the foundation of the Society, also had associations with Olney. William Bull, the Independent, frequently preached there.

It is curious that both Newton, the curate of Olney parish church, and Dr. Moses Browne, its vicar, had a very unorthodox start to their careers. Newton had made a number of voyages in slave ships, and Browne, originally a pen-cutter, began his career as a writer with a theatrical tragedy *Polidus, or Distress'd Love*, and a farce *All Bedevl'd, or the House in a Hurry*. There is a tablet to his memory in Olney church. Newton and his wife are buried in the churchyard, and a number of late seventeenth-century tombstones there were carved by the Olney mason, James Andrews, who taught Cowper to draw.

The Decorated church, with its tall spire, is believed to be the work of a Northamptonshire designer. It is a noble building with unusually beautiful tracery in the chancel windows. The spire rises from a cornice of masks and flowers.

Among other clergymen associated with Olney church were Thomas Scott, the Biblical commentator, who succeeded Newton as curate at Olney, and was afterwards rector of Aston Sandford; and Henry Gauntlett, vicar from 1815 to 1834, whose son, Henry, became famous as a composer and editor of psalm and hymn-tunes. He played the organ in Olney church from the age of nine, and in later life was noted for reforming the construction of church organs. It was through his exertions that the C organ became firmly settled in England. He attained a high reputation as an organist, and was chosen by Mendelssohn to play the organ part in *Elijah* on its first production in 1846, at the Birmingham Festival. Thomas Collingridge, who founded the famous London firm which became the proprietors of the *City Press*, printed his first bills at Olney in 1833. It was his son, Mr. W. H. Collingridge, who gave Cowper's house to the town of Olney as a museum.

North-west of Olney is Cowper's Oak, the original of *Yardley Oak*. In Cowper's day it measured 22 feet 6½ inches in girth, and it remained a sturdy veteran until the summer of 1949, when it was badly damaged by children, who lighted a fire in the hollow trunk. Fortunately 'Judith', now known as 'Gog', which was 28 feet 5 inches round when Cowper measured it, and the only slightly smaller 'Magog', both in Yardley Chase near Chase Farm, are still in good condition.

After nineteen years in Olney, which were, on the whole, both happy and productive, Cowper and Mrs. Unwin moved to Weston Underwood, a mile and a quarter from Olney, to the larger house offered to them by the Throckmortons. They formed many new friendships before finally leaving Buckinghamshire nine years later, with the regret expressed in the lines Cowper wrote on the window shutter of his bedroom, and still to be seen there:

> Farewell, dear scenes, for ever closed to me;
> Oh! for what sorrows must I now exchange ye.

Forebodings only too fully realized.

Although Weston Lodge, with its memories of Cowper, remains, the mansion of his kind friends was pulled down in 1836, when the last of the Throckmorton family, who had been seated there since 1446, left their old home.

This great Roman Catholic family had many distinguished members, some of whom suffered greatly for their religion. Robert died on a pilgrimage to the Holy Land in 1518; another Robert fought for the King in the Civil War and had his estates sequestrated, but his son regained them. Yet another Robert was a Roman Catholic non-juror, famous for his charity and benevolence, who died in 1720.

Only the gateposts of the park, and the stables, crowned with a cupola, now remain of their house, but the Roman Catholic chapel they built in 1838 has a black-and-white pavement from the entrance hall of the old Weston House, and occupies part of its site. It is now a private house.

The modern manor-house stands near the older site, and the park, with its splendid avenues of lime, beech, elm, and chestnut trees, is now open to the public.

The church was refounded in 1368. The tower was added in the middle of the fifteenth century. There is a considerable quantity of old glass, a fifteenth-century font, a fourteenth century inscription to John Olney, whose family held the manor before the Throckmortons, and murals to the Throckmortons and to the Higgins family, who lived at Turvey Hall over the Bedfordshire border.

ii

All the countryside round Olney has been happily de-
lineated by Cowper in his verses, particularly in *The Task*,
where line after line conjures up the enchanting views which
are still to be seen. Every coign of vantage has its view described, every loved spot is enshrined, to shed the magic of
his contemplative poetry over the scenes we too can see and
learn to love. His verses do not scale the heights, perhaps,
but they are so perfectly suited to the quiet landscape they
describe that their charm will never fade.

Ravenstone, which lies about a mile west of Weston
Underwood, is a remote village of thatched stone cottages
on the side of a grassy valley, with seventeenth-century brick
almshouses neighbouring the church. It was granted to the
Giffards at the Conquest, and passed through various hands
until Henry III granted it to his Poitevin favourite, Peter de
Chaceporc, who died at Boulogne in 1254, and under his
will left six hundred marks to found a house of regular
canons, to be chosen from Merton in Surrey. The following
year the King carried out his wishes, founding an Augus-
tinian Priory at Ravenstone.

The priory was dissolved in 1625, and lands at Ravenstone
were granted to Cardinal Wolsey the following year. It
eventually came into the possession of Sir Moyle Finch, and
remained in the hands of this exceptionally able family.
Sir Moyle's widow was created Viscountess Maidstone and
Countess of Winchelsea, and her younger son Heneage became Lord Chancellor of England and Earl of Nottingham.

The church stands on a little hill, with Abbey Farm below
marking the site of the vanished priory, and a moated
orchard which probably marks the site of the old manor-
house. The church is mainly Early English, with considerable alterations made in the seventeenth century when the
Finch chapel was built. The monument to the first Earl of

Nottingham, who died in 1689, was long attributed to Cibber, but is now believed by some authorities to be the work of Joseph Catterns. The Earl's effigy, in white marble, lies in a semi-recumbent attitude on a colossal four-posted bed, with black marble pillars supporting an elaborate canopy, and with white marble curtains tied to the bed-posts. The Finch chapel has a contemporary oak screen, and there is a considerable amount of seventeenth-century woodwork in the church.

In the churchyard is the grave of Thomas Seaton, who was vicar from 1721 to 1741. He was a hymnologist, and by his will founded the Seatonian Prize for sacred poetry at Cambridge. A wall tablet was erected to him in 1932.

iii

Cowper often walked to Clifton Reynes, where his friend Thomas Jones was curate, and he could talk happily to Mrs. Jones's sister, Lady Austen. It is still a compact flowery little village, remote from the bustle of modern life down a winding lane which stops dead at the church overlooking the Ouse.

Although the church is small, the blending of various periods since the twelfth century, and the many remarkable fourteenth-century details, make it well worth a visit. There is a splendidly carved fourteenth-century font, and sedilia, and two interesting black wooden effigies dating from about 1300. Two other effigies carved in oak are probably those of Ralph de Reynes, lord of the Manor, and his wife Amabel, and date from about 1320. Wooden effigies are extremely rare in England, and nowhere else are there four in one church. They are the only examples in Bucks. There are also fourteenth-century effigies in stone, and fifteenth-century brasses, to members of the de Reynes family. The knight in the fourteenth-century monument, who has not been identified with certainty, rests his feet on a beautifully sculptured dog, with its name, Bo, on its collar. Cut round the base of the tomb is a pageant of contemporary costume.

There are also several marble tablets to the Small family, who purchased the manor in 1750, including a bust by Scheemakers. Not the least surprising is an inscription to 'Samuel Pepys, died 1703, most faithful rector of this church'. Although he died in the same year as the diarist, there appears to have been no connexion between them.

The rectory Cowper so often visited remains unaltered, but the manor-house was destroyed about 1850, and only a garden-wall, orchard, fish-pond, and part of an avenue remain to mark its site, although the fine seventeenth-century circular dovecote still stands in the centre of the village. The Robin Hood Inn, and several of the houses in the village, date from the seventeenth century.

North of Olney the Wellingborough road leaves Buckinghamshire soon after passing the hamlet of Warrington, the highway running between Northampton and Bedford. Lavendon, which lies a mile or two eastward along the Bedford road, is the most northerly place in the county. It is a large village clustering round its interesting church, but was once of much greater importance, with a castle and abbey, which have long vanished, though there are traces of a moat which once surrounded the abbey, founded for Præmonstratensians in the twelfth century. The seventeenth-century Grange is said to have been built with some of the material from the abbey buildings. The lane running northeast from the main road leads to a farmhouse on a mound, which marks the site of the castle, of which very little is known, as it had disappeared even by Leland's time.

In the south of the village, beside the river, is Lavendon Mill, which probably marks the site of the Norman mill, and on the east is the manor-house of Uphoe, which was owned by the family of Norwich for 400 years, and is still surrounded by a circular moat. It is now a farm-house.

By far the most important building surviving in Lavendon is the church, which has a considerable amount of Saxon work in the chancel, nave, and tower. The fifteenth-century font is delicately carved, and there is a Jacobean pulpit, and a mahogany chair with the heads of mastiffs carved on it, probably of early eighteenth-century work. There are numerous memorials to vicars. Robert Newton, the founder of Hertford College, Oxford, died at Lavendon Grange in 1753. He was a kinsman of Sir Isaac Newton, the scientist, who was a frequent visitor at the Grange.

Farther along the Bedford road is Cold Brayfield, right on the county boundary.

Cold Brayfield was part of the wide possessions of the Countess Judith, niece of the Conqueror, after whom the Yardley Oak was named. Her second husband was King David of Scotland, who was recognized as Earl of Huntingdon in right of his marriage, and the overlordship of these lands seems to have fluctuated between the descendants of her first and second husbands, according to the fortunes of war or peace between Scotland and England, until the thirteenth century. In 1343 Waterhall in this parish was held by the family of Grey, by sergeanty, minutely defined as that of sending a man to the wars in Wales 'on a horse without a saddle, price 40d., one bow without a cord, and one arrow without a head, when required by the king', surely a strangely Gilbertian ordinance?

A Georgian house with fine grounds sloping down to the Ouse, a farm, an ancient but not particularly interesting church, and a handful of cottages, make up the whole of this old-time possession of the Scots Kings.

Newton Blossomville is the last village on the Ouse before it finally flows out of Bucks. If its simple stone houses are not so typical of Buckinghamshire as could be wished for our last sight of the county, it is at least a village of considerable charm and individuality, with the reedy river lapping the churchyard walls, and stonecrop and houseleek decorating many a nook and cranny in the village. The church is a mixture of styles, and its red chancel roof looks rather incongruous against the grey walls. It has been thoroughly restored, but has a fifteenth-century font, a late seventeenth-century pulpit, a ringer's gallery, and some fragments of fourteenth-century glass.

Half a mile away is Newton Park, once the seat of the lords of the manor, but now a farm. The second part of the name of Newton Blossomville is derived from the family of de Blosseville, who held land here as tenants of the Countess Judith.

Beyond Newton Blossomville the Ouse branches out into innumerable small streams, which wander into Bedfordshire, less than a mile away, and we may well leave the county with Cowper's lines in mind:

> '... we have borne
> The ruffling wind scarce conscious that it blew,
> While admiration feeding at the eye,
> And still unsated, dwelt upon the scene!
>
> .   .   .   .   .
>
> Scenes must be beautiful which daily view'd
> Please daily, and whose novelty survives
> Long knowledge and the scrutiny of years;
> Praise justly due to those that I describe.'

INDEX